THE GLORY OF CHRIST

THE TREASURES OF JOHN OWEN

THE GLORY OF CHRIST

Abridged and made easy to read by
R.J.K. Law

THE BANNER OF TRUTH TRUST

THE BANNER OF TRUTH TRUST
3 Murrayfield Road, Edinburgh EH12 6EL
P.O. Box 621, Carlisle, Pennsylvania 17013, USA

*

© R. J. K. Law 1994
First Published 1994
ISBN 0 85151 661 0

*

Typeset in 10½/13pt ITC New Baskerville
Printed in Great Britain by
BPC Paperbacks Ltd
A member of
The British Printing Company Ltd

Publisher's Preface

The Puritan era in seventeenth-century England was distinguished pre-eminently by the rich school of evangelical authors whose writings have had such a powerful influence wherever they have been read. Among these men none has been regarded more highly than John Owen, whose works combine biblical insight, theology with spirituality, and experimental religion to such a marked degree. As an indication of the value placed upon him by the present publishers it may be noted that the sixteen volumes of his *Works* (in the Goold edition of 1850-53) have been kept in print on account of their importance ever since they were reprinted in 1965. It is hoped that this availability of the full text of Owen can be continued; the abridgements which are now being issued are not intended to be a replacement.

Those who have accused Owen of being hard to read have generally been people who lacked the time to read him as he deserves. But considering the extent of his writings even those who wish to read him more fully have often, for the same reason, been unable to become as familiar with him as they would wish. Many cannot read enough to be able to determine which of his books contain his finest work and there can be few alive who have read him at all. As a result many of Owen's most important and relevant treatises are little known today. The Rev R.J.K. Law, the abridger of this text, began his work purely for his own profit and as a memory aid. As he proceeded, he felt more and more like the men of 2 Kings chapter 7 who, discovering the riches of the deserted camp of the Syrians, exclaimed, 'This day is a day of good tidings, and we hold our peace.' The need of others to share in his findings thus led to a change in his original purpose.

After examining the quality and skill of Dr Law's abridgements we have fully shared his enthusiasm for putting the best of Owen into the hands of a far larger number of Christians.

The present abridgement is the third to be published in the series *The Treasures of John Owen.* Those who have already expressed appreciation for the earlier volumes will be encouraged to learn that more of Owen's work has been prepared in similar form by Dr Law and it is expected that further abridgements will be forthcoming in due course.

In *The Glory of Christ* we meet the writings of Owen at their richest and most mature. He focuses our attention on Christ, the heart of the gospel. Owen himself tells us that the substance of the work began in his own private meditation and study and only later was shared with his congregation. Here, then, is a master theologian writing about the things, or better, the person, nearest to his heart. The work itself was composed almost at the end of Owen's life and first published in 1684, the year after his death. Indeed, the material in chapters fifteen to seventeen of this abridgement appeared for the first time in the second edition of 1696, having been found among Owen's papers only after his death but clearly intended as the closing section of the work.

On the day of Owen's death (24 August 1683) William Payne, a minister in Saffron Walden who had accepted responsibility for seeing the manuscript of this work through to publication, visited him in Ealing (now part of London) to share the good news that *Meditations on the Glory of Christ* was now going through the press. Owen's biographers record his memorable and beautiful reply: 'I am glad to hear it; but, O brother Payne! the long-wished-for day is come at last, in which I shall see that glory in another manner than I have ever done, or was capable of doing in this world.' It is clear from these pages that Owen had already seen the glory of Christ from afar and pondered long on its significance. His teaching is well-suited to bring us to share in his longing to know Christ better, to see his glory more clearly and to serve him more faithfully. It is the conviction of the publisher that many readers will discover this book to be one of the hidden treasures of Christian literature and will return to it again and again for instruction and spiritual refreshment.

In this abridgement the Bible is quoted throughout in the *New King James Version*.

Contents

	Publisher's Preface	v
1	Seeing Christ's Glory	1
2	Christ's Glory as God's Representative	11
3	The Glory of Christ in His Person	28
4	The Glory of Christ's Humbling Himself	38
5	The Glory of Christ's Love as Mediator	50
6	The Glory of Christ's Work as Mediator	57
7	The Glory of Christ's Exaltation	63
8	The Glory of Christ under the Old Testament	69
9	The Glory of Christ's Union with the Church	74
10	The Glory of Christ's Giving Himself to Believers	82
11	The Glory of Christ in Restoring All Things	91
12	The First Difference between Beholding the Glory of Christ by Faith and by Sight	100
13	The Second Difference between Beholding the Glory of Christ by Faith and by Sight	109
14	The Third Difference between Beholding the Glory of Christ by Faith and by Sight	122
15	Exhortation to Unbelievers	127
16	How to Recognize Spiritual Decay in the Soul	141
17	How the Soul may be Recovered from Spiritual Decays	160

I: *Seeing Christ's Glory*

When the high priest under the law was about to enter the holy place on the day of atonement, he took in his hands sweet incense from the golden table of incense. He also had a censer filled with fire taken from the altar of burnt-offerings, where atonement was made for sin with blood. When he actually entered through the veil, he put the incense on the fire in the censer until the cloud of its smoke covered the ark and the mercy-seat (*Lev.* 16:12-13). The reason why he did all this was to present to God, on behalf of the people, a sweet smell from the sacrifice of propitiation.

Corresponding to this mystical type, the great High Priest of the church, our Lord Jesus Christ, prayed when he was about to enter the holy place not made with hands (*John* 17). His glorious prayer, set alight by the blood of his sacrifice, filled the heavens above, the glorious place of God's residence, with a cloud of incense, that is, the sweet smell of his blessed intercession. By the same eternal fire by which he offered himself a bloody sacrifice to make atonement for sin, he kindled in his most holy soul those desires, that all the benefits of his sacrifice should be given abundantly to his church.

The greatest desire that Christ expressed in his prayer was that his people might be with him to behold his glory (*John* 17:24). It is clear that in this prayer the Lord Christ was referring to his own glory and the actual sight of it

(*John* 17:4-5). He is not concerned that his disciples should merely see how glorious he was, but that the beholding of his glory might bring encouragement, strength, satisfaction and blessedness to his disciples. This was the whole reason why his mediatory glory was given to him. When Joseph had revealed himself to his brothers, he charged them that they should tell his father of all his 'glory in Egypt' (*Gen.* 45:13). He did not do this to boast of his own glory, but because he knew how happy and satisfied his father would be when he knew in what a glorious position his son was. Similarly, the Lord Christ desired that his disciples should see his glory in order that they might be filled with joy and happiness for evermore.

Only a sight of his glory, and nothing else, will truly satisfy God's people. The hearts of believers are like a magnetized needle which cannot rest until it is pointing north. So also, a believer, magnetized by the love of Christ, will always be restless until he or she comes to Christ and beholds his glory. The soul which can be satisfied without beholding the glory of Christ, that cannot be eternally satisfied with beholding the glory of Christ, is not a soul for whom Christ prays.

We can now lay down a great foundational truth: One of the greatest privileges the believer has, both in this world and for eternity, is to behold the glory of Christ. So Christ prays that 'they may behold my glory'. But this glorious privilege is not to be limited to the heavenly state only. It includes the state of believers in this world as I shall show.

Unbelievers see no glory in Christ. They see nothing attractive about him. They despise him in their hearts.

Outwardly they cry, like Judas, 'Hail, Master', but in their hearts they crucify him. Thus they strip him of his glory, deny the 'only Lord that bought us' and substitute a false Christ. Others think little of Christ and his glory and see no use for his person in Christianity—as though there were anything in our religion which has any truth or reality apart from Christ!

In the early days of the church there were swarms of brain-sick persons who vomited out many foolish ideas culminating at length in Arianism, in whose ruins they now lie buried. The gates of hell in them did not prevail against the rock on which the church is built. As it was said of Caesar, 'He alone went soberly about the destruction of the commonwealth', so many still oppose the person and glory of Christ under the pretence that nothing can be believed except that which reason can understand and accept. Indeed, unbelief in the Trinity, and the incarnation of the Son of God, the sole foundation of Christianity, is so spread about in the world, that it has almost demolished the life and power of true Christianity. And not a few who dare not let people know what they really believe lead people to think they love Jesus, when all the time they scorn, despise and persecute those who truly desire to know nothing but Christ and him crucified.

But God, in his appointed time, will vindicate his honour and glory from the foolish attempts of sinful men who attempt to strip him of both. Meanwhile, it is the duty of all those who 'love the Lord Jesus in sincerity' to testify to his divine person and glory according to the ability God has given to each of us, and this I have chosen to do, not in a controversial way, but in order to strengthen the faith

[3]

of true believers, to build them up in the knowledge of Christ and his glory and to help them experience that which they have, or may have, of the power and reality of these things.

That which I intend to show is, that beholding the glory of Christ is one of the greatest privileges that believers are capable of in this world, or even in that which is to come. Indeed, it is by beholding the glory of Christ that believers are first gradually transformed into his image, and then brought into the eternal enjoyment of it, because they shall be 'for ever like him', for they 'shall see him as he is' (*2 Cor.* 3:18, *1 John* 3:1-2). On this depend our present comforts and future blessedness. This is the life and reward of our souls (*John* 14:9, *2 Cor.* 4:6).

Scripture shows us two ways by which we may behold the glory of Christ. We may behold it by faith in this world, faith being 'the evidence of things not seen', and we may behold it by sight in the next (*2 Cor.* 5:7-8, *1 Cor.* 13:12).

When Christ prayed 'that they may behold my glory', he meant by actual sight in the light of eternal glory. But the Lord Jesus does not exclude that sight of his glory which we may have by faith in this world; rather he prays for the perfection of it in heaven. So we can learn the following lessons:

No man shall ever behold the glory of Christ by sight in heaven who does not, in some measure, behold it by faith in this world. Grace is a necessary preparation for glory and faith for sight. The soul unprepared by grace and faith is not capable of seeing the glory of Christ in heaven. Many will say with confidence that they desire to be with Christ and to behold his glory. But when asked, they can give no reason for this desire, except that it would be better than going to hell. If a man claims to love and desire that which he never even saw, he is deceiving himself.

In this way Roman Catholics are deceived. They delight outwardly in images of Christ depicting his sufferings, resurrection and glory. By these images they think their love for him and delight in him grows more and more strong. But no man-made image can truly represent the person of Christ and his glory. Only the gospel can do that.

John writes not only of himself but of his fellow apostles also, 'We beheld his glory, the glory as of the only begotten of the Father, full of grace and truth' (*John* 1:14). Now what was this glory of Christ which they saw, and how did they see it?

It was not the glory of Christ's outward condition for he had no earthly glory or grandeur. He kept no court, nor did he entertain people to parties in a great house. He had nowhere to lay his head, even though he created all things. There was nothing about his outward appearance that would attract the eyes of the world (*Isa.* 52:14; 53:2-3). He appeared to others as a 'man of sorrows'.

Neither was it the eternal essential glory of his divine nature that is meant, for this no man can see while in this world. What we shall see in heaven we cannot conceive.

What the apostles witnessed was the glory of 'grace and truth'. They saw the glory of Christ's person and office in the administration of grace and truth. And how did they see this glory? It was by faith and in no other way, for this privilege was given only to those who 'received him' and

[5]

believed on his name (*John* 1:12). This was the glory which the Baptist saw when he pointed to Christ and said, 'Behold! the Lamb of God who takes away the sin of the world!' (*John* 1:29).

So, let no one deceive himself. He that has no sight of Christ's glory here shall never see it hereafter. The beholding of Christ in glory is too high, glorious and marvellous for us in our present condition. The splendour of Christ's glory is too much for our physical eyes just as is the sun shining in all its strength. So while we are here on earth we can behold his glory only by faith.

Many learned men have written of this future state of eternal glory. Some of their writings are filled with excellent things which cannot but stir the minds and hearts of all who read them. But many complain that such writings do nothing for them. They are like a man who 'beholds his natural face in a mirror, and immediately forgets what he saw' (*James* 1:23-4). These writings make no fixed impression on their minds. They briefly refresh, like a shower of rain in a drought, which does not soak down to the roots. But why do these writings make no impression on them? Is it not because their idea of future things has not arisen out of an experience of them which faith alone gives?

In fact, a soul will be troubled rather than edified when it thinks of future glory, if it has had no foretaste, sense, experience or evidence of these things by faith. No man ought to look for anything in heaven if he has not by faith first had some experience of it in this life. If men were convinced of this, they would spend more time in the exercise of faith and love about heavenly things than they usually do. At present they do not know what they enjoy, so they do not know what to expect. This is why men who are complete strangers to seeing the person and glory of Christ by faith have turned to images, pictures and music to help them in their worship.

So it is only as we behold the glory of Christ by faith here in this world that our hearts will be drawn more and more to Christ and to the full enjoyment of the sight of his glory hereafter.

It is by beholding the glory of Christ by faith that we are spiritually edified and built up in this world, for as we behold his glory, the life and power of faith grow stronger and stronger. It is by faith that we grow to love Christ. So if we desire strong faith and powerful love, which give us rest, peace and satisfaction, we must seek them by diligently beholding the glory of Christ by faith. In this duty I desire to live and to die. On Christ's glory I would fix all my thoughts and desires, and the more I see of the glory of Christ, the more the painted beauties of this world will wither in my eyes and I will be more and more crucified to this world. It will become to me like something dead and putrid, impossible for me to enjoy.

For these and other reasons, I shall first ask how we behold the glory of Christ by faith. Then I will try and lead believers into the more retired walks of faith, love and holy meditation, showing them how to behold the glory of Christ by faith. To encourage such study, consider the blessings it will bring us: the rewards of this glorious duty.

By beholding the glory of Christ we shall be made fit and ready for heaven. Not all who desire to go to heaven are fit and ready for it. Some are not only unworthy of it and excluded from it because of unforgiven sin; they are not prepared for it. Should they be admitted, they would never enjoy it. All of us naturally regard ourselves as fit for eternal glory. But few of us have any idea of how unfit we really are, because we have had no experience of that glory of Christ which is in heaven. Men shall not be clothed with glory, as it were, whether they want to be or not. It is to be received only by faith. But fallen man is incapable of believing. Music cannot please a deaf man, nor can beautiful colours impress a blind man. A fish would not thank you for taking it out of the sea and putting it on dry land under the blazing sun! Neither would an unregenerate sinner welcome the thought of living for ever in the blazing glory of Christ.

So Paul gives 'thanks to the Father who has qualified us to be partakers of the inheritance of the saints in light' (*Col.* 1:12). Indeed, the first touches of glory here, and the fullness of glory hereafter, are communicated to believers by an almighty act of the will and the grace of God. Nevertheless, he has ordained ways and means by which they may be made fit to receive that fullness of glory which still awaits them, and this way and means is by beholding the glory of Christ by faith, as we shall see. Knowing this should stir us up to our duty, for all our present glory lies in preparing for future glory.

By beholding the glory of Christ we shall be transformed 'into the same image' (*2 Cor.* 3:18). How this is done and how we become like Christ by beholding his glory, will become clear as our study progresses.

By beholding the glory of Christ by faith we shall find rest to our souls. Our minds are apt to be filled with troubles, fears, cares, dangers, distresses, ungoverned passions and lusts. By these our thoughts are filled with chaos, darkness and confusion. But where the soul is fixed on the glory of Christ then the mind finds rest and peace for 'to be spiritually minded is peace' (*Rom.* 8:6).

By beholding the glory of Christ we shall begin to experience what it means to be everlastingly blessed. 'We shall always be with the Lord' (*1 Thess.* 4:17). We shall 'be with Christ', which is best of all (*Phil.* 1:23). For there we shall 'behold his glory' (*John* 17:24). And by seeing him as he is, 'we shall be made like him' (*1 John* 3:2). This is our everlasting blessedness.

The enjoyment of God by sight is commonly called the 'Beatific Vision', and it is the only motive for everything we do in that state of blessedness. What the sight of God is and how we will react to it, we cannot imagine. Nevertheless we do know this, that God in his immense essence is invisible to our physical eyes and will be in eternity just as he will always be incomprehensible to our minds. So the sight which we shall have of God will be always 'in the face of Jesus Christ' (*2 Cor.* 4:6). In Christ's face we shall see the glory of God in his infinite perfections. These things will shine into our souls filling us for ever with peace, rest and glory.

We can rejoice in these things even though we cannot understand them. We can talk of them but never fully comprehend them. In fact, true believers experience a foresight and foretaste of this glorious condition. Sometimes, when reading and meditating on the Bible our hearts are filled with such a sense of the uncreated glory of God shining through Jesus Christ that we experience unspeakable joy. So arises that 'peace of God which passes all understanding', which keeps 'our hearts and minds through Jesus Christ' (*Phil.* 4:7). 'Christ' in believers 'the hope of glory' (*Col.* 1:27) gives them a foretaste of that future glory. And where any have no acquaintance with these things, they are blind and dead to spiritual things. It is because believers are lazy and ignorant that we do not experience more and more in our souls the visits of grace and the dawnings of eternal glory.

In the following chapters we will consider the following questions: What is that glory of Christ which we can behold by faith? How do we behold the glory of Christ by faith? And how is our beholding Christ by faith different from our actually seeing his glory in heaven?

2: *Christ's Glory as God's Representative*

The glory of Christ is the glory of the person of Christ. So he calls it 'that glory which is mine', which belongs to me, to my person (*John* 17:24).

The first glorious thing we learn about the person of Christ is that he is the perfect revelation of the Father. This revelation of the Father is for the benefit of the church, for we behold 'the glory of God in the face of Jesus Christ' (*2 Cor.* 4:6).

The glory of God includes both the holy properties of his nature and the things he has purposed to do. The only way we can know these things of God is 'in the face' or person 'of Jesus Christ', for he is 'the image of God' (*2 Cor.* 4:4). He is 'the brightness of the Father's glory, and the express image of his person' (*Heb.* 1:3). He is 'the image of the invisible God' (*Col.* 1:15).[1]

But Christ is specially glorious because he and he alone perfectly reveals God's nature and will to us. Without Christ we would have known nothing truly about God for he would have been eternally invisible to us. We would never have seen God at any time, either in this life or the next (*John* 1:18).

In his divine person, Christ is the essential image of God the Father. He is in the Father and the Father in him, both existing in the unity of the same divine essence (*John*

1   Owen deals with this theme in detail in his work on the person of Christ, also to be published in this series.

14:10). Furthermore, he is with the Father, as well as being the essential image of the Father (*John* 1:1, *Col.* 1:15, *Heb.* 1:3). But when he assumed human nature he became the representative of God's image to the church, so that only by Christ do we understand the wonderful and excellent things of God's nature and will (*2 Cor.* 4:6). Without Christ, God would still be to us the 'invisible God'. We see the glory of God only in the person of Christ.

This is the glory which the Father gave him, and which by faith we may behold. He alone makes known both to angels and men the essential glory of the invisible God, without which a perpetual comparative darkness would have covered all creation.

The foundation of our religion, the rock on which the church is built, the ground of all our hopes of salvation, of life and immortality, is the revelation that is made of God's nature and will by Jesus Christ. So if Christ fails, if he, the Light of the world becomes darkness, then we are for ever lost. But if this Rock stands firm, the church is safe and shall be triumphant for ever.

It is as the representative of God that the Lord Christ is exceedingly glorious. Those who cannot see his glory by faith do not know him. When they worship him, they worship an image of their own devising. Not to see that Christ is the only true representative of the glory of God to the souls of men, is to be an unbeliever. This was the sad state of the unbelieving Jews and Gentiles of old. They did not, they would not, they could not, behold the glory of God in him and that was why they did not believe in him (see *1 Cor.* 1:21-25). The one who does not see the wisdom and power of God and all the other holy properties of the divine nature in Christ as well as seeing in him the only way of salvation is, to put it bluntly, an unbeliever.

The essence of faith lies in glorifying God (*Rom.* 4:20). But we cannot do this without the revelation of the glorious qualities of his divine nature. These qualities and glories of the divine nature are revealed to us by Christ alone.

It is only by Christ that we can glorify God rightly and acceptably. Hence the great purpose of the devil, when the gospel was first preached, was to blind the eyes of men's understanding, and to fill their minds with prejudices so that they might not behold his glory (*2 Cor.* 4:3-4). By various deceitful ways he attempted to hold on to his title 'god of this world'. By counterfeiting supernatural appearances of power and wisdom, he laboured to prejudice the minds of men and so to turn them away from the glorious light of the gospel which proclaimed to all that the Lord Christ was the perfect and only true revealer of God's image. This blindness is taken away from the minds and hearts of believers only by the almighty power of God; for Paul tells us that God who commanded the light to shine out of darkness, has shone in our hearts with 'the knowledge of the glory of God in the face of Jesus Christ' (*2 Cor.* 4:6). The unbelieving world of Jews and Gentiles perished under this darkness; so do all present day unbelievers who deny that Jesus is truly God as well as being truly man. But if Christ were only a man he could never have truly represented God to us for no mere creature can ever truly represent the divine nature.

Since men fell from God by sin, a great part of their misery and punishment is that their minds are covered

[13]

with thick darkness and so they are ignorant of the true nature of God. They do not know him and they have never seen him. So this promise was given to the church: 'For behold the darkness shall cover the earth, and deep darkness the people; but the Lord will arise over you, and His glory will be seen upon you' (*Isa.* 60:2).

The ancient philosophers had many ideas about the Divine Being. They boasted that they were the only wise men in the world (see *Rom.* 1:22). But Paul assures us that the world in its wisdom did not come to know God (*1 Cor.* 1:22). Indeed he calls these philosophers, atheists, or men 'without God in the world' (*Eph.* 2:12).

They were atheists because they had no certain guide to lead them infallibly to know the divine nature. All they had were their own systems of logic and their wild ideas (*Rom.* 1:21). The best they could do was to 'feel after God', like men groping in the dark (*Acts* 17:27).

It is a fact that their best ideas of invisible and incomprehensible things did not and could not free them from idolatry, immorality and other gross sins. Paul explains this at length in Romans 1:18-32.

Men may claim they have a light within them, that the power of reason is able to lead them to the knowledge of God so that they may live lives pleasing to him. But without divine revelation they are no better than those described by Paul.

Concerning this worldwide darkness, that is, the ignorance of God in men's minds, Christ is called, and indeed is, the 'Light of men', the 'Light of the world', because in him and by him alone this darkness is dispelled. He is the 'Sun of Righteousness'.

This ignorance of God, of his nature and will, was the reason why evil entered the world and why it continues to prevail in the world. On this ignorance of God Satan set up his kingdom. He exalted himself, by virtue of this darkness, in the place of God as the object of all religious worship. For the things which the Gentiles sacrificed, they sacrificed to devils, and not to God (*1 Cor.* 10:20, *Lev.* 17:7, *Deut.* 32:17, *Ps.* 106:36, *Gal.* 4:8). This is how the devil wields the power and sceptre of his kingdom in the minds of the 'children of disobedience'.

Ignorance of God is the source of all wickedness and confusion among men. From this ignorance arose that flood of abominations which God swept away in Noah's day. The sins of Sodom and Gomorrah were burned up with 'fire from heaven'. In short, all the rage, blood, confusion, desolations, cruelties, oppressions and disasters which fill the world to this day, by which the souls of men have been swept into eternal destruction, have all arisen from the ignorance of God.

We are the descendants of those described. Our forefathers were given up to as brutish a service of the devil as any nation under the sun. It was therefore the work of infinite mercy that the day dawned on us, and that the 'day-spring from on high has visited us'. God might justly have left us to perish in the blindness and ignorance of our forefathers. But of his own will, and by his own powerful grace alone, he has 'translated us out of darkness into his marvellous light'. But the horrible ingratitude of men for the glorious light of the gospel, and the abuse of it, will bring on us his severe judgements.

God was known under the Old Testament by the revelation of his Word, and the institutions of his worship. This was the glory and privilege of Israel, as the psalmist declares (*Ps.* 147:19-20). The church knew him but only as he dwelt in 'thick darkness', because they had no full and clear revelation of him (*Exod.* 20:21, *Deut.* 5:22, *1 Kings* 8:12, *2 Chron.* 6:1). The reason why God kept them in the dark about himself was to teach them how imperfect their state was. It could not lead them to understand that glory which should later be revealed. But in Christ we see that 'God is light and in him is no darkness at all'.

Even though darkness then covered the earth, and gross darkness the people concerning the knowledge of God, yet there was twilight in the church. The day had not yet dawned. The 'shadows had not fled away', nor had the 'day-star shone' in the hearts of men. But the 'Sun of Righteousness' arose in all its strength and beauty, when the Son of God appeared in the flesh. In Christ, God himself, his Being and the mystery of his existence in three distinct persons, was gloriously revealed to believers, and the light of the knowledge of these truths dispelled all those shadows that were in the church, and also pierced the darkness which was in the world, so that none could continue to be ignorant of God but those who would not see (see *John* 1:5, 14, 17-18, *2 Cor.* 4:3-4).

It is as the representative of such a God that Christ is glorious. So we need to learn how to see the glory of God in the face of Jesus Christ. He calls to us, saying, 'Behold me! Look to me and be saved!' (*Isa.* 45:22). But what shall we see in Christ? Do we see him as 'the image of the invisible God', representing God's nature and will to us? Do we see him as 'the express image' of the person of the Father, so that we have no need to ask with Philip, 'Lord show us the Father', because, having seen him, we have seen the Father also (*John* 14:9)? To see Christ so as to see God in him—that is to behold his glory, that glory which we ought to long to see and make every effort to see. But if we do not see it, we are still in darkness. Though we say we see, we are blind like others.

Remember how David longed and prayed for a sight of this glory (*Ps.* 63:1-2). In the sanctuary there was an obscure representation of the glory of God in Christ. How much more, then, ought we to treasure that view of it which we may have with open face, even though we still see it 'as in a mirror' (*2 Cor.* 3:18).

Moses also desired to see the glory of God (*Exod.* 33:18). He knew that the ultimate rest, blessedness and satisfaction of the soul does not come from seeing the works of God, but from seeing the glorious God himself. And if we have a right understanding of future blessedness, we cannot but have the same desire to see more of his glory in this life. But the question is: How? Left to ourselves we shall come to the same conclusion that Agur came to that we are stupid (see *Prov.* 30:2-4).

It is in Christ alone that we may have a clear idea of the glory of God. The Father appointed him to be the true representation of his glory (see *John* 1:18; 14:7-10, *2 Cor.* 4:6, *Col.* 1:15, *Eph.* 3:4-10, *Heb.* 1:3). That glory is wonderfully displayed in both his wisdom and his love.

Infinite wisdom is one of the most glorious properties of the divine nature. The way God's glory is revealed in creation, providence and most wonderfully in Christ, was planned by infinite wisdom. As wisdom is an essential property of the divine nature we can have no understanding of it, we can only worship and adore it from that infinite distance which separates us from God. But we can know it by its works, the most glorious of which is the great work of the salvation of the church, as Paul says (*Eph.* 3:9-10).

All the treasures of this wisdom are hidden, laid up and revealed in Christ. By faith, believers see it in Christ, whereas unbelievers do not (*1 Cor.* 1:22-24). In beholding the glory of this infinite wisdom of God in Christ, we behold Christ's own glory also, the glory given him by his Father. This is the glory of Christ, that in and by him alone the wisdom of God is revealed and truly represented to us. When God appointed Christ as the great and only means by which his glory could be represented, he gave him honour and glory above all creation. Compared with Christ, all creation reveals little of God's infinite wisdom. We have only to see how men abused the revelation of God's wisdom in creation to see how insufficient was that revelation compared to the revelation of God's infinite wisdom revealed in Christ. To see this fills the souls of believers 'with joy inexpressible and full of glory' (*1 Pet.* 1:8).

Love is another glorious property of the divine nature. John tells us that 'God is love' (*1 John* 4:8). This is a wonderful revelation of the divine nature. Love casts out envy, hatred, malice and revenge with all the rage, fierceness, implacability, persecution and murder that these evil passions produce. These do not belong to God, for 'God is love'. But how shall we behold the glory of this love? It is hidden to all, in God himself. The natural ideas of the love of God, even in the wisest philosophers, are corrupt, weak and imperfect. Generally men think that God's love is easy-going, overlooking sin.

Paradoxically the works of God's providence some-times prevent us from having a right view of God's love, for though it is true that 'God is love', yet 'his wrath is revealed from heaven against all ungodliness of men'. All things are daily filled with evidences of his anger and displeasure. How then can we behold the glory of God's love? John tells us: 'In this the love of God was manifested toward us, that God has sent His only begotten Son into the world, that we might live through him' (*1 John* 4:9). This is the only sure evidence that God is love. So the divine nature is made known to us in the mission, person and offices of the Son of God. Without this we remain ignorant of this divine love.

So we may see how excellent, how beautiful, how glorious and desirable he is as the representation of God's loving nature. He who does not behold the glory of Christ as the representation of God's love is utterly ignorant of these heavenly mysteries. He does not know either God or Christ. He has neither the Father nor the Son. He does not know God, because he does not know the holy prop-erties of his nature in the chief way designed by infinite wisdom for their revelation. He does not know Christ because he does not see the glory of God in him. So, what-ever ideas men may have gleaned from nature or from the works of providence that there is love in God, yet from them no one can know for sure that 'God is love'. Apart from Christ no man can come to a true understanding of God's love.

These things are the deep things of God which belong

to that mystery of God's wisdom. Those who are unspiritual cannot receive it, as Paul tells us (*1 Cor.* 2:14). If, then, you would behold the glory of Christ as the great means of being sanctified and comforted, and as the only way you can be made fit and ready to behold his glory in eternal blessedness, consider what is represented and made known to you of God in Christ, in whom God purposed to glorify himself.

All that may be known of God for our salvation, especially his wisdom, love, goodness, grace and mercy on which the life of our souls depends, are represented to us in all their splendour in and through Christ. No wonder then that Christ is glorious in the eyes of believers!

Many people look on Christ merely as a teacher come from God to reveal his will and to teach us how to worship him, and so indeed he was. But they say that this was the only reason why he came. This is the teaching of Islam. They do not see that he is the great and only representative of the glory of the divine nature. This glory of Christ they despise and reject, because in their ignorance they do not believe that he is truly God as well as being truly man.

But I ask those whose minds are better attuned to heavenly things, Why do you love Jesus Christ? Why do you trust in him? Why do you honour him? Why do you desire to be in heaven with him? Can you say why? If one of your reasons is that in him you behold by faith the glory of God which otherwise would have been eternally hidden from you, especially the glory of his love in sending Christ to atone for your sins, then he is indeed precious to you.

It is our duty and our privilege to behold the glory of Christ. But today, many who call themselves Christians are strangers to this duty. Our Lord Jesus Christ told the Pharisees that in spite of all their boasting, they did not know God. They had no real acquaintance with him, no spiritual view of his glory. And it is the same with us. In spite of so many claiming to know Christ, yet few behold his glory, few are transformed into his image and likeness.

Some talk much of imitating Christ and following his example. But no man will ever become 'like him' by trying to imitate his behaviour and life if they know nothing of the transforming power of beholding his glory. The truth is that most of us are woefully defective in this, and many are discouraged because thoughts of this glory of Christ seem too high or too hard. But is not the real cause our own lack of spirituality?

If we regularly beheld the glory of Christ our Christian walk with God would become more sweet and pleasant, our spiritual light and strength would grow daily stronger and our lives would more gloriously represent the glory of Christ. Death would be most welcome to us.

Is Christ, then, glorious in our eyes? Do we see the Father in him? Do we daily meditate on the wisdom, love, grace, goodness, holiness and righteousness of God as revealed to us in Christ? Do we realize that to see this glory in heaven will be our everlasting blessedness? Does the sight of his glory which we have here increase our desire for that perfect sight of it we shall one day have of it above?

It may be said, 'I do not understand these things and anyway I am not concerned about them.' But nothing is more clearly and fully revealed in the gospel than that Jesus Christ is 'the image of the invisible God', that in seeing him we see the Father also, that we have 'the light of the knowledge of the glory of God in the face of Jesus Christ'. This is the chief, fundamental mystery and truth of the gospel, which, if it is not received and believed will make all other truths useless to our souls.

In fact, the light of faith is given to us chiefly to enable us to behold the glory of God in Christ (*2 Cor.* 4:6). If we do not have this light which is given to believers by the power of God, we must be strangers to the whole mystery of the gospel. But when we behold the glory of God in Christ, we behold Christ's glory also. This is how the image of God is renewed in us, and how we are made like Christ.

Anyone who thinks that this is unnecessary to Christian practice and for our sanctification does not know Christ, nor the gospel. Nor has he the true faith of the universal church. This is the root from which all Christian duties arise and grow and by which they are distinguished from the works of heathens. He is not a Christian who does not believe that faith in the person of Christ is the source and motive of all evangelical obedience or who does not know that faith rests on the revelation of the glory of God in Christ. To deny these truths would overthrow the foundation of faith and would demolish the Christian religion. So it is our duty daily to behold by faith the glory of Christ.

But to those who are strangers to this mystery yet are not enemies to it, I give the following advice.

(i) Make up your mind that to behold the glory of God by beholding the glory of Christ is the greatest privilege which is given to believers in this life. This is the dawning of heaven. It is the first taste of that heavenly glory which God has prepared for us, for this is eternal life, to know the Father and Jesus Christ whom he has sent' (*John* 17:3). Unless you value this as a priceless privilege, you will not enjoy it. We are to 'cry after this knowledge, and lift up our voice for this understanding'.

(ii) As it is a great privilege, so also it is a great mystery which requires much spiritual wisdom to come to a right understanding of it and to practise it aright (*1 Cor.* 2:4-5). Flesh and blood will not reveal it to us. We must be taught by God if we would understand it (*John* 1:12-13, *Matt.* 16:16-17). Mere unsanctified reason will never enable us to understand how to go about this duty, nor guide us in that understanding.

We are not so foolish as to think we can learn a trade without the diligent use of helps. Shall we think that we may become spiritually skilful and wise in the understanding of this mystery without making any real effort to use the helps God has given us? The most important of them is fervent prayer. Pray with Paul that 'the eyes of your understanding may be enlightened to behold' the glory of God in Christ. Pray that the 'God of our Lord Jesus Christ, the Father of glory, may give to you the spirit of wisdom and revelation in the knowledge of him'. Fill your minds with spiritual thoughts of Christ. Lazy souls do not get the tiniest sight of this glory. The 'lion in the way' deters them from making the slightest effort.

(iii) Learn how to behold the glory of Christ by remembering how you once set your mind on worldly things. Sinful, unregenerate people filled with lustful desires continually think about and conjure up in their minds those objects which satisfy their desires until their 'eyes become full of adulteries, and they cannot cease from sinning'. If they work as hard as that to feed their lusts, shall we not work just as hard in beholding that which transforms our minds into Christ's likeness, so that the eyes of our understanding shall be continually filled with his glory? Then when we actually see him we shall behold him without any interruption and we shall never cease to delight in him and to love him.

(iv) This is the only way to behold the glory of God without which we have nothing of the power of religion in us, whatever we may claim. Go to the whole creation, and they will say, 'We have heard the fame and report of these things', and what we have heard we declare. But we have so little understanding of these things. 'The heavens declare the glory of God, and the firmament shows his handiwork.' 'The invisible things of God are understood by the things that are made, even his eternal power and Godhead.' But how little do we learn from creation compared to what we behold of them in Christ Jesus.

How blind to these things was the best ancient philosopher compared to the lowliest of the apostles, indeed to the least in the kingdom of heaven!

But we must not rest satisfied with only an idea of this truth or a bare assent to the doctrine. Its power must stir our hearts. What is the true blessedness of the saints in heaven? Is it not to behold and see the glory of God in Christ? Does it not fill them with inexpressible joy and delight? And do we expect, do we desire the same state of blessedness? If so, then know that it is our present view of the glory of Christ which we have by faith that prepares us for that eternal blessedness.

These things may be of little use to some who are babes in spiritual knowledge and understanding or who are unspiritual or lazy and not capable of understanding these divine mysteries (see *1 Cor.* 3:1-2, *Heb.* 5:12-14). That is why Paul declared this wisdom of God in a mystery to them that were perfect, that is, who were more advanced in spiritual knowledge who had had their 'senses exercised to discern both good and evil' (*Heb.* 5:14). It is to those who are experienced in the meditation of invisible things, who delight in the more retired paths of faith and love, that they are precious.

There are several implications from what has been said:

(i)   In Christ we behold the wisdom, goodness, love, grace, mercy and power of God all working together for the great work of our redemption and salvation. The wisdom and love of God are in themselves infinitely glorious. But we cannot see how glorious they are except in the redemption and salvation of the church which is achieved only in and by Christ. Then the beams of their glory shine on us with unspeakable comfort and joy (*2 Cor.* 4:6). So Paul, seeing the glories of infinite wisdom and knowledge in the redemption and salvation of the church, breaks out in a paean of praise in Romans 11:36: 'For of him and through him and to him are all things, to whom be glory for ever. Amen.'

(ii)   We believe in God only in and through Christ. This is the life of our souls. God himself, whose nature is infinitely perfect, is the highest object of our faith. But we cannot come directly to God by faith. We must come by the way and by the helps he has appointed for us. This is the way by which he has revealed his infinite perfections to us, which is Jesus Christ who said, 'I am the way . . . No one comes to the Father except through me.' By our faith in Christ we come to put our faith in God himself. And we cannot do this in any other way but by beholding the glory of God in Christ, as we have seen.

(iii) This is the only way by which we may come to know God as Saviour and Sanctifier of our souls. Without this representation of the glory of God in 'the face of Jesus Christ', every beam of divine light that shines on us, every spark that arises from the remains of the light of nature within us, only succeeds in disturbing the minds of men rather than leading them to the saving knowledge of God. A flash of light in the dark giving only a momentary sight of objects only confuses rather than helps a traveller. It leaves him more likely to wander in the wrong direction. Such were all those ideas of the Divine Being which those who boasted themselves to be wise among the heathen embraced. Their views of God did not transform them into his image and likeness, as the saving knowledge of Christ does (*Col.* 3:10).

So Paul shows up the foolishness of this world's wisdom, both of the Jews who sought a sign and the Greeks who sought wisdom but without Christ (*1 Cor.* 1:20-24). It was made clear to all the world that the 'wise' and the 'scholar' were, in the purpose of God, left to their own wisdom, to their natural light and reason. But in spite of all their efforts they did not, could not, come to the knowledge of God or of his salvation. Then, in their pride and arrogance, they treated with contempt the only way by which God did reveal himself. They considered it weak and foolish. So having shown all their wisdom to be fool-ishness, it pleased God to establish the only way by which he and his salvation may be truly known, that is, by and in Christ Jesus.

3: *The Glory of Christ in His Person*

The second thing in which we may behold the glory of Christ, given to him by his Father, is the mystery of his person. He is God and man in one person. In him are two distinct natures, the one, eternal, infinite, immense, almighty, the form and essence of God; the other having a beginning in time, finite, limited, confined to a certain place, which is our nature. This nature he took to himself when he was 'made flesh, and dwelt among us'.

This is a glory whose beams are so wonderful that the blind world cannot see their light and beauty and so many deny the incarnation of God. Nevertheless, this is the glory of our religion, the glory of the church, the only rock on which it was built, the only source of present grace and future glory.

This is that glory which the angels long to behold, the mystery they 'desire to look into' (*1 Pet.* 1:12). This desire of theirs was represented by the cherubim in the most holy place of the tabernacle, which were symbols of the ministry of angels in the church. The ark and the mercy-seat were a type of Christ carrying out his work. These cherubim were made standing over them, as being in heaven above, but earnestly looking down upon them in a posture of reverence and adoration. And in their beholding of the glory of Christ lies no small part of their eternal blessedness.

In addition, this glory is the ruin of Satan and his kingdom. Satan's sin, as far as we can see, consisted of two evils. Firstly, there was his pride against the person of the Son of God by whom he was created (*Col.* 1:16). This was the start of his transgression. Secondly, there was his envy against mankind, made in the image of God, the Son of God the first-born. This completed his sin. Nothing was now left for him to lift himself proudly up against, nor to vent his malice on. To Satan's eternal confusion and ruin, God in his infinite wisdom united both the natures he had sinned against in the one person of the Son, who was the first object of his pride and malice. By this, his destruction is accompanied with everlasting shame in the revelation of his foolishness in attempting to overthrow infinite wisdom, as well as his misery in being overthrown himself by the power of the two natures united in one person.

This is the glory on which lies the foundation of the church. The foundation of the whole of creation was laid in an act of absolute sovereign power, when God 'hung the earth on nothing'. But the foundation of the church is on this mysterious, immovable rock of the union of the divine and human natures in one person, Jesus Christ, the Son of the living God. Here the whole church must fall down and worship the God who laid this wonderful foundation.

In Exodus 3:2-6, we read how the Angel of the Lord appeared to Moses in a flame of fire out of the midst of a bush. This fire was a living representation of the presence of God in the person of the Son. Concerning the Father, Christ is called the Angel of the Lord, the Angel of the covenant. But absolutely in himself, he was the 'God of

Abraham, Isaac and Jacob'. The fire represented his divine nature which is as a 'consuming fire'. The fire also pictured his present work which was to deliver his church out of a fiery trial. This fire was in a bush, where it burned, but the bush was not destroyed. And although the fire was in the bush only for a short while, yet God was said to dwell in the bush (*Deut.* 33:16). The fire in the bush, which was there only temporarily, was a type of him in whom 'the fullness of the Godhead dwelt bodily', and that for ever (*Col.* 2:9). The eternal fire of the divine nature dwells in the bush of our frail nature, yet our frail nature is not destroyed. So God dwells in this bush, with all his goodwill towards sinners.

Moses was amazed at this marvellous and wonderful sight. But if the sight of the burning bush was so wonderful, how much more wonderful is the reality in Christ Jesus. Moses was told to 'take off his shoes'. By this we are taught to cast away all fleshly ideas and desires, so that we may behold this glory, the glory of the only begotten of the Father, purely by faith.

(i)   Let us get it fixed in our minds that this glory of Christ in his divine-human person, is the best, the most noble and beneficial truth that we can think about or set our hearts on.

What are all other things in comparison to the 'knowledge of Christ'? Paul considers them but 'refuse' (*Phil.* 3:8-10). If that is not so for us then we are sadly unspiritual. What does the world think about and desire most? The psalmist tells us: 'There are many who say, "Who will show us any good?"' (*Ps.* 4:6). Who will help us to get as much of this world's goods as will give rest and satisfaction to our minds? By contrast, the psalmist says, 'Lord, lift up the light of your countenance upon us.' The light of the glory of God in the face of Jesus Christ is the only good which will satisfy me and which I desire.

The Scripture takes to task the foolishness of men who 'spend their money for that which is not bread, and their labour for that which does not do us any real good'. They spend their time and money chasing after perishing things, when something solid and everlasting is set before them. What do men think about most of the time? Some spend their time planning how to make provision for the flesh and how to satisfy its lusts (*Rom.* 13:14). They spend their thoughts on sinful pleasures, refusing to behold the glory of Christ. Some continually worry about the things of this world, seeking promotion and rewards for all they do. So they are transformed into the image of the world, becoming earthly, unspiritual and stupid. The blindness, the darkness, the foolishness of poor sinners! Do they realize who it is they despise? Do they realize who it is they are rejecting and for what?

Others are of a more noble mind and spend their time meditating on the works of creation and providence. This is a work worthy of our nature. But in all these there is no glory to be compared with the glory of Christ's person. (Compare *Ps.* 8 with *Heb.* 2:5-6. See also *Pss.* 73:25; 89:6.)

(ii)   Let us diligently study the Bible and the revelations of the glory of Christ revealed there. This is what Christ himself tells us to do (see *John* 5:39) and the prophets in the Old Testament show us how to do it (see *1 Pet.* 1:11-13).

When we read Scripture we must always bear in mind

that the revelation and doctrine of the person of Christ and his office are the foundation of all that we learn from the prophets and apostles (*Eph.* 2:20-22, *Luke* 24:26-27, 45-46). Deny this and the Scriptures no longer become to us a revelation of the glory of God in the salvation of the church. The Jews are an example of those who deny this truth (*2 Cor.* 3:13-16).

There are, therefore, such revelations of the person and glory of Christ treasured up in the Scriptures, whose heights and lengths and breadths and depths shall never be fully discovered or understood in this life. And it is in meditating on these divine revelations that much of the life of faith rests.

There are three ways by which the glory of Christ is represented to us in Scripture.

(a) By direct descriptions of his glorious person and incarnation. (See *Gen.* 3:15, *Pss.* 2:7-9; 45:2-6; 68:17-18; 110, *Isa.* 6:1-4; 9:6, *Zech.* 3:8, *John* 1:1-3, *Phil.* 2:6-8, *Heb.* 1:1-3; 2:14-16, *Rev.* 17:16.)

(b) By prophecies, promises and clear instructions concerning him, all leading our thoughts to behold his glory.

(c) By the sacred institutions of divine worship under the Old Testament. Their whole purpose was to represent to the church the glory of Christ in the carrying out of the work he was sent to do.

Take, for instance, his personal appearances under the Old Testament which showed forth his glory. Such was the vision which Isaiah had, 'when he saw his glory, and spoke of him'. Isaiah saw a representation of the glory of the divine presence of Christ filling his human nature, the temple of his body, with a train of all glorious graces. And if what Isaiah saw was so glorious that even the seraphim could not bear to look at the sight, how much more glorious is Christ himself openly revealed in the gospel!

And what about the glory which his three disciples saw on the Mount of Transfiguration of which Peter speaks (*2 Pet.* 1:17-18)? There God gave Christ honour and glory, which all those who believe in him should behold and admire, not only those who heard this testimony with their physical ears, but all who read the Scriptures. We are all obliged to search for and to meditate on the glory of Christ. From the throne of his majesty, by audible voices, by visible signs, by the opening of the heavens, by the descent of the Holy Spirit on him, God testified to Jesus as his eternal Son. In all these, God gave him the honour and glory which has often filled the hearts of many with joy and delight.

So, in reading and studying the Bible, we ought to make every effort to search for the revelations of the glory of Christ in it as did the prophets of old. The glory of Christ is the 'pearl of great price' which we should make every effort to find (*Matt.* 13:45-46). And the Scripture is the ocean into which we dive to discover this pearl, or the mine in which we dig for its precious treasures (*Prov.* 2:1-5). Every sacred truth that reveals something of the glory of Christ to our souls, is a pearl or precious stone which enriches us. But when the believer discovers this pearl of great price itself, then his soul cleaves to it with joy.

The glory of Scripture is that it is the great, indeed, the only outward means for us to know the glory of Christ.

(iii) Having come to the light of the knowledge of the

glory of Christ from Scripture or by the preaching of the gospel, let us regard it as our duty to meditate frequently on his glory. It is the neglect of meditation that keeps so many Christians in a feeble state, regardless of their privileges. They hear of these things and assent to the truth of them or at least they do not question them. But they never solemnly meditate on them. They think that meditation is above their capabilities, or they are totally ignorant of how to go about it, or they are not too concerned about it, or they treat it as fanaticism. Many cannot meditate because their minds are so cluttered up with earthly things. The mind must be spiritual and holy, freed from all earthly clutter. It must be raised above things here below if we wish to meditate on the glory of Christ. So many are strangers to this duty because they do not mortify their earthly desires and concerns.[1]

There are some who profess to be strict, disciplined Christians, but who never put aside time to meditate on the glory of Christ. Yet they tell us that they desire nothing more than to behold his glory in heaven for ever. They are being wholly inconsistent. It is impossible that someone who never meditates with delight on the glory of Christ here in this world, who does not make every effort to behold it by faith as it is revealed in Scripture, should ever have any real gracious desire to behold it in heaven. It is sad, therefore, that many can find time to think much on earthly, foolish things, but have no heart, no desire to meditate on this glorious object. What is this faith and love they claim to have?

[1] Owen discusses this topic with his usual thoroughness in his work *On Spiritual Mindedness* in *Works*, volume 7.

(iv) Let your thoughts of Christ be many, increasing more and more each day. He is never far from us as Paul tells us (*Rom.* 10:6-8). The things Christ did were done many years ago and they are long since past. 'But', says Paul, 'the word of the gospel where these things are revealed, and by which they are brought home to our souls, is near us, even in our hearts, that is, if we are true believers and have received the word by faith.' So the gospel exhibits Christ and all the benefits of his mediatory work to us. If, therefore, the Word is in our hearts, Christ is near us. If we at any time turn into ourselves, to converse with the Word in us by meditation, we shall find him ready to receive us into communion with himself. By the light of the knowledge of Christ which we have by the Word, unexpected thoughts of him will continually come to mind. But if our minds and hearts are filled with other things, how can we expect to have fellowship with him in beholding his glory?

So, to show us how near he is to us, we are told that 'he stands at the door, and knocks', ready to enter our souls and have communion with us (*Rev.* 3:20). And Christ is always accompanied with the glorious train of his graces. If these are not received, he is not received. You may boast of knowing Christ, but if there is no evidence of his grace in your heart and life then your boasting is foolish. But to those to whom Christ is the hope of future glory, he is also the life of present grace.

Sometimes it may seem that he has withdrawn from us. We cannot hear his voice, nor see his face, nor experience any sense of his love even though we diligently seek him. In this state, all our thoughts and meditations concerning

Christ will be barren and fruitless, bringing no spiritual refreshment to our souls. If we are happy with such life-less, fruitless thoughts of him which bring no awareness of his love, nor give us any sight of the glory of his person, the power of religion in us will wither away. Our duty is fully expressed by the spouse in the Song of Solomon (*Song of Sol.* 3:1-4; 5:2-8). When in such a state we must dili-gently seek him in prayer, meditation, mourning, reading and hearing his Word in all ordinances of divine worship both in private and in public.

But generally, Christ is near believers and is ready to receive them. Faith continually seeks him and thinks of him, for in this way Christ lives in us (*Gal.* 2:20). It is some-times said about two people that one lives in the other. This cannot happen except where their hearts are so knit together that both night and day each lives in the other's thoughts. So ought it to be between Christ and believers. He dwells in them by faith. But we experience the power of his life in us only as our thoughts are filled with him and we continually delight in him. If, therefore, we would behold the glory of Christ, we must be filled with thoughts of Christ and his glory on all occasions and at all times. This is the mark of a true Christian.

(v) Let all our thoughts concerning Christ and his glory be accompanied with admiration, adoration and thanksgiving. When he comes again, it will be to be 'admired in all who believe' (*2 Thess.* 1:10). When believ-ers see Christ at his second coming they shall be filled with overwhelming admiration at his glorious appearance. And this admiration will result in adoration and thanksgiving (see *Rev.* 5:9-14).

So, when, by faith we behold the glory of Christ as we meditate on his divine-human person, we should not see him merely as glorious in himself. We must, rather, make every effort to let that glory so fill our hearts with love, admiration, adoration and praise to him that our souls will be transformed into his image.

Let us, then, make up our minds to be more heavenly minded or we will never relish the idea of beholding the glory of Christ.

4: *The Glory of Christ's Humbling Himself*

'There is one God', says Paul, 'and one mediator between God and man, the man Christ Jesus' (*1 Tim.* 2:5). In that great separation between God and man caused by our sin and apostasy which of itself could result in nothing but the utter ruin of the whole human race, there was none in heaven or earth who was fit or able to reconcile them and bring about a righteous peace between them. Yet this must be done and could be done only by a suitable mediator.

This mediator could not be God himself as God only, for a mediator does not mediate for only one. But if he was God then he could be said to be biased, for there is only one God and man is not God. Man needs a mediator to represent him just as God needs a mediator to represent him (*Gal.* 3:20). So whatever God might do in the work of reconciliation, yet as God he could not do it as mediator.

As for man, there was no creature in heaven or earth fit to undertake this work. For 'if one sins against another, God will judge him. But if a man sins against the Lord, who will intercede for him?' (*1 Sam.* 2:25). As Job said, 'Nor is there any mediator between us who may lay his hand on us' (*Job* 9:33).

In this state of things, the Lord Christ, as the Son of God, said, 'Behold, I have come to do your will, O God' (*Heb.* 10:7). By taking our nature into union with himself, in his own divine person, he became in every way fit and able for this work and so undertakes it. How then may we behold the glory of Christ as mediator? We may behold it in his humbling himself to take up this office of mediator, in his carrying it out, and in its results.

We may behold the glory of Christ in his infinite willingness to humble himself to take this office of mediator on himself, and uniting our nature to his for that purpose. He did not become mediator by chance. Nor was it imposed on him against his will. He did not have to become mediator. He freely chose to become mediator. He willingly humbled himself in order that he might make a righteous peace between God the Judge and man the sinner.

Christ, being in the form of God, says Paul, willingly took on himself the form of a servant. He willingly humbled himself. He willingly made himself of no reputation and was obedient even to the death of the cross (*Phil.* 2:5-8). It is this willingness to humble himself to take our nature into union with himself which is glorious in the eyes of believers.

Such is the transcendent glory of the divine nature, that it is said of God that he 'dwells on high', and yet 'humbles himself to behold the things that are in the heavens and in the earth' (*Ps.* 113:4-6). God is willing to take notice of the most glorious things in heaven and the lowliest things in the earth. This shows his infinite humility.

Consider the infinite distance between God's essence, nature or being, and that of his creatures. So all nations before him 'are as the drop of a bucket, and are counted as the small dust of the balance'. Indeed, they are as nothing. They are counted to him as less than nothing and foolishness. Who can measure the distance between that which is infinite and that which is finite? It cannot be done. So, the infinite, essential greatness of the nature of God, with his infinite distance from the nature of all creatures, means that God has to humble himself to take notice of things infinitely below him.

God is so infinitely high and lofty, so inhabits eternity in his own eternal being, that it is an act of mere grace in him to take notice of things infinitely below him. Therefore he does it in a special way. He does it by taking special notice of those whom the world despises, 'the humble and contrite ones' (*Isa.* 57:15).

God is infinitely self-sufficient both in himself and in all that he does. Man is continually seeking for self-satisfaction. But no creature can find eternal blessedness or satisfaction in itself, for no creature is self-sufficient. Not even Christ's human nature in heaven is self-sufficient. It lives in God and God in it. It continues to exist in full dependence on God and continually receives blessed and glorious communications from him. God alone lacks nothing and stands in need of nothing. Nothing can be added to him to increase his blessedness, seeing he 'gives to all life, breath and all things' (*Acts* 17:25). No creature can contribute one mite to God's eternal blessedness. He is infinitely perfect in his own nature (*Job* 35:6-7).

How glorious then is this willingness of the Son of God to humble himself to be our mediator. What heart can conceive, what tongue can express the glory of that mind of Christ which brought him down from infinite glory to take our nature into union with his so that he could mediate with God on our behalf?

In order to behold the glory of Christ as mediator better, let us consider the special nature of this willingness of his to humble himself. In doing this we must first consider what he did not do when he humbled himself to be our mediator.

(i)   Christ did not lay aside his divine nature. He did not cease to be God when he became man. The real glory of his willingness to humble himself lies in this great truth, that 'being in the form of God, he did not consider it robbery to be equal with God' (*Phil.* 2:6). That is, being really and essentially God in his divine nature, he declared himself to be equal with God, or with the person of the Father. He was 'in the form' of God, that is, he was God. He was partaker of the divine nature, for God has no form or shape. So he was equal with God, in authority, dignity and power. Because he was in the form of God, he must be equal with God, for though there is order in the divine persons, there is no inequality in the Divine Being. So the Jews clearly understood his meaning when he said God was his Father. They knew he meant that he was equal with God. For when he said this, he also claimed equal power with the Father in all his divine works. He said, 'My Father has been working until now, and I have been working' (*John* 5:17).

Being in the form of God, he took the form of a servant, and was found in fashion as a man (*Phil.* 2:7). This is his infinite humility. Paul does not say that he stopped being God, but though continuing to be God, he took 'the form of a servant'. That is, he took our nature upon him. He became what he was not, but he did not cease to be what he always was (see *John* 3:13). Although he was then on earth as Son of man, yet he was still God, for in his divine nature he was still also in heaven.

He who is God, can never not be God, just as he who is not God can never be God. The difference between us and the Socinians[1] is this, that we believe that Christ, being God, was made man for our sakes, whereas they teach that Christ, being only a man, was made a god for his own sake.

This, then, is the glory of Christ's willingness to humble himself. This is the life and soul of all heavenly truth and all heavenly mysteries, namely, that the Son of God, becoming in time what he was not, that is, Son of man, did not cease thereby to be what he was, even the eternal Son of God.

(ii) Christ did not convert his divine nature into the human. This was what some Arians of old taught, and some still say today that the 'Word which was in the beginning', by which all things were made, was in the fullness of time turned into flesh, that is, the substance of the divine nature was turned into flesh as the water in Christ's miracle was turned into wine. By an act of divine power it ceased to be water and was now wine only, not water mixed with wine. So these men suppose a substantial change of the one nature into the other, that is, the divine nature was changed into the human in the same way that Roman Catholics imagine the bread and wine become the body and blood of Christ by transubstantiation.

But this doctrine destroys both of Christ's natures, and leaves him a person who can no longer be our mediator.

1   The Socinians, disciples of Faustus and Laelius Socinius in the 16th century, like contemporary Unitarians and Jehovah's Witnesses, denied the true and eternal deity of Christ.

For, according to this teaching, that divine nature in which he was in the form of God ceased to be God. Indeed, it was completely destroyed because it was substantially changed into the nature of man as the water ceased to be water when it was turned into wine. And that human nature which was made by the transformation of the divine nature into the human has no relationship to us, seeing it was not 'made of a woman', but of the substance of the Word.

(iii) The humbling of Christ to be our mediator did not change or alter the divine nature. Eutyches (378-454) and those that followed him taught that the two natures of Christ, the divine and the human, were mixed and compounded as it were into one. But this could not happen without the divine nature being altered, for it would be made to be essentially what it was not, for one nature has but one and the same essence.

But as we said before, although the Lord became what he was not before, in that our nature was made to be his, yet his divine nature always remained the same. In the divine nature there is neither 'variableness nor shadow of turning'. It remained the same in him, in all its essential properties and in all its blessedness as it was from eternity. The Lord Christ did and suffered many things both in his life and in his death as a human being. But all that he did and suffered as a human being was done and suffered by his whole person, even although what he did and suffered as a human being was not actually done and suffered by his divine nature. Because his human nature was part of his whole person, what he did as a human being could be said to have been done by himself as God, e.g. God purchased his church 'with his own blood' (*Acts* 20:28).

(iv) What did the Lord Christ do with his divine nature when he willingly humbled himself to become man? Paul tells us that he 'humbled himself, and made himself of no reputation' (*Phil.* 2:7-8). He veiled the glory of his divine nature in ours, so that there was no outward appearance or revelation of it. The world could not see that he was the true God, so it believed he was not a good man in claiming to be God. So when Christ said, 'Before Abraham was, I am', which asserted his pre-existence from eternity in another nature than what they could see, they were filled with rage, and 'took up stones to cast at him' (*John* 8:58-59). They gave as the reason for their madness that 'he, being a man, should make himself to be God' (*John* 10:33). They could not understand that one and the same person could be both God and man. It was beyond their fleshly reason. Nothing in creation had two natures.

But this difficulty is solved by the glory of Christ in his humiliation, for although in himself, in his own divine person, he was 'over all, the eternally blessed God' (*Rom.* 9:5), yet he humbled himself for the salvation of the church. To the eternal glory of God, he took our nature and was made man. Those who cannot see a divine glory in his doing this neither know him, nor love him, nor believe in him, nor in any way belong to him.

So, because these people cannot behold the glory of Christ in this humbling of himself to take our nature, they deny the foundation of our religion, namely the divine person of Christ. If he is willing to be made man, then he shall be treated only as a man and no more. So they reject the glory of God's infinite wisdom, goodness and grace which concerns him more than does his whole creation. And they dig up the root of all evangelical truths which are nothing but branches growing from it.

To the world, our Lord Jesus Christ is a 'stumbling-block and a rock of offence'. If we should say he was only a prophet, no more than a man sent from God, there would be no opposition from the world. The Moslems and the Jews both say he was only a man, a prophet sent from God. The hatred of the Jews for Christ was because he professed himself to be God, and as such was believed on in the world. And today, there are many who are willing to say he was a prophet sent from God, who do not, who will not, who cannot, believe the mystery of his willingness to humble himself to take our nature into union with his divine nature, nor see the glory of it. But take this away, and all our religion is taken away with it. Farewell to the mystery, the glory, the truth and the power of Christianity! Let a refined heathenism be set up in its place. But this is the rock on which the church is built, and against this rock the gates of hell shall not prevail.

(v) Christ's humbling of himself to be our mediator was not by means of some ethereal substance forming a phantasm or an appearance only. One of the first heresies that assailed the church was the Docetic heresy.[2] The Docetics taught that all that was done or suffered by Christ as a man was done or suffered by one who only appeared to be a man. His appearance as a man was like the appearance of angels in the shape of men, eating and drinking under the Old Testament. So there was only an appearance of Christ in the man Jesus at Jerusalem, in whom he

---

[2] Thus named from the Greek verb 'to appear'.

suffered no more than in other believers. But this heresy was dealt with by the early church telling these heretics that an imaginary Christ gives an imaginary salvation.

We must, then, consider the true nature of this glorious divine humiliation that Christ willingly undertook in order to be our mediator. The essence of the biblical teaching is as follows: The eternal person of the Son of God, or the divine nature in the person of the Son, did, by a wonderful act of his divine power and love, take our nature into union with himself, that is, to be his own even as the divine nature is his own.

This is the infallible foundation of faith, even to those who can understand very little of these divine mysteries. They can and do believe that the Son of God took our nature to be his own, so that whatever was done in that nature was done by him as a true human being would do it. The Lord Christ took that nature which is common to all men into union with his divine nature in his own person, so that it became truly his and he was truly the man Christ Jesus. This was the mind that was in him.

In this assumption of our nature in which he lived and suffered, by which he was found in fashion as a man, the glory of his divine person was veiled, and he made himself of no reputation. But this I have already dealt with.

We must also take note, that in taking human nature into union with his divine nature, Christ did not change it into a divine, spiritual nature, but preserved it in its entirety, with all its essential human properties and abilities. So Christ really lived and suffered, was really tried, tempted and forsaken in his true human nature, just as any other man might have so lived and suffered. He was exposed to all earthly evils just as every other man is.

The glory of Christ's humiliation was the result of the divine wisdom of the Father as well as of the love of the Son. It was the highest evidence of God's loving care towards his sinful human creatures. What can be compared to it? It is the glory of Christianity and the life-giving power of all evangelical truth. It lifts up the mystery of the wisdom of God above the reason or understanding of men and angels so that it becomes the object of faith and wonder only. It is a mystery that exalts the greatness of God. Considering the infinite distance between God and his creation, it is not surprising that all his works and ways cannot be understood by his creatures (*Job* 11:7-9, *Rom.* 11:33-36).

It is of this great mystery that that great promise concerning him is given to the church. 'He will be as a sanctuary' (namely to all believers as Peter tells us, *1 Pet.* 2:7-8), 'but a stone of stumbling and a rock of offence.' To whom? To those who 'stumble, being disobedient to the word, to which they also were appointed' (*Isa.* 8:14, *1 Pet.* 2:8).

Christ is a sanctuary, a sure refuge to all that put their trust in him. And what would a troubled man fleeing to a safe place be looking for? He would look for all his needs to be met, to be delivered from all his fears, to be protected from all dangers. Such is the Lord Christ to all sin-distressed souls.

Christ is a refuge to us in all our spiritual sorrows and troubles (*Heb.* 6:18). Are you burdened with a sense of sin? Are you weighed down under the oppression of any spiritual enemy? Do we, as a result of any of these things, 'walk in darkness and have no light'? One look at the glory of Christ will strengthen and comfort us.

When we go to someone for help, two questions arise. The first is, Is the person to whom we are going for help *willing* to help us, and secondly, Is he *able* to help us? We need to know that Christ is both willing and able to help us and to meet all our needs.

We may well ask, What will Christ *not* do for us? He who emptied and humbled himself, who came down from the infinite height of his glory to take our finite nature into union with his infinite nature, will he not meet all our needs and answer according to his infinite wisdom all our prayers for help? Will he not do all that is necessary for us to be eternally saved? Will he not be a sanctuary for us? We have no reason to fear his ability and power, for in becoming man he lost nothing of his power as the Almighty God, nor of his infinite wisdom and glorious grace. He could still do all that he could do as God from eternity. So Christ is indeed most willing and able to help us. And if we do not see his glory in this, it is because we have no faith in us.

But to unbelievers and the disobedient who stumble at the Word, Christ is a 'stone of stumbling and a rock of offence'. They cannot, they will not see the glory of Christ's infinite willingness to humble himself to take our nature upon him. They have no desire to see it. They hate and despise it. It is offensive to them. So they choose to deny completely that he is God rather than admit that he humbled himself for our sakes. Rather than admit this glory, they will allow him no glory. They say he was merely a man and that this was his only glory. This is the principle of darkness and unbelief which works so effectively in the minds of many. They think it absurd that one person can be both man and God. So they see no glory in Christ and find no refuge or safety in him. But it is just here that faith triumphs against them. Faith sees that to be a glorious sanctuary which unbelief cannot see.

So I exhort you to spend much time meditating on the glory of Christ in his humiliation. Unless we are diligent in this, it is impossible to keep our faith steadily fixed on Christ or be ready for self-denial and taking up our cross, for the humbling of Christ is the chief motive for this duty (*Phil.* 2:5-8). And no man denies himself rightly, who does not consider the self-denial of the Son of God. For what are the things of which we are to deny ourselves? Is it not our goods, our rights and freedoms, our relations and our lives? They are perishing things from which, whether we like it or not, death will separate us. But the glory of Christ is for ever. Believers will never be separated from it. So if you find yourself at any time unwilling to part with this world, then lift up your eyes and by faith behold the glory of Christ who 'made himself of no reputation'.

5: *The Glory of Christ's Love as Mediator*

It was because Christ loved us that he became our mediator. And it was because the Father loved us that he appointed his Son to be the mediator between God and man for the redemption and salvation of the church. And this love of the Father for us was 'before the foundation of the world' (*Eph.* 1:4). The Father's love is seen in his eternal election of a part of mankind to be brought into the eternal enjoyment of himself, through the mystery of the blood of Christ, and the sanctification of the Spirit (*2 Thess.* 2:13-16, *Eph.* 1:4-9, *1 Pet.* 1:2). Election, being the eternal act of the will of God the Father, is founded on divine love for the following reasons:

Election reveals the glory of God's nature which is love, for 'God is love' (*1 John* 4:8-9). The love of God is the foundation of our redemption and salvation. So election, being an eternal act of the will of God, cannot be based on anything but that which is in God himself, and if we could look into all the treasures hidden in God's wonderful nature, we would find none to which election could be truly attributed but love.

Election is founded on divine love because it is free and undeserved. We did nothing to persuade God to choose us rather than others. Any good done to us which is altogether undeserved and which is done to promote our good, is an act of love and cannot be anything else. Any good there is in God's people is the result of election and not the reason why God chose us. The only thing that moved God to choose us was his undeserved love.

The fruits or results of election are inexpressible acts of love. It is by many acts of love that election is brought to fruition, actually bringing about the salvation of all those whom God chose to save (*John* 3:16, *Jer.* 31:3, *Eph.* 1:3-5, *1 John* 4:8-9, 16).

It was because God chose to save a people out of this sinful human race that Christ's office as mediator became necessary. And it was because the Son of God loved us that he was willing to become our mediator and so the whole purpose of the Father's love was to be carried out by Christ.

In order to understand the love of the Son for the elect we must first note the following:

The whole number or society of the elect were creatures made in the image of God, and were therefore loved by God. All that they were, had, or hoped for, came from God's goodness and love. The very life of their soul depended on their love of God shown by perpetual obedience to his will. And what a happy state this was— preparing themselves for the eternal life of love in heaven!

From this state they fell by sin into a state of enmity with God. This brought upon them all miseries and sorrows both in this life and for ever. But in spite of this terrible catastrophe, our nature was able to be restored to its original enjoyment of God. So the first act of the love of Christ towards the elect was pity and compassion. A creature made in the image of God, and fallen into misery, yet capable of being restored, is truly an object of divine compassion and pity. But there can be no compassion or pity shown to those who can never be recovered. So the Lord Christ did not show compassion or pity to the angels that fell, because their nature could not be restored (see *Heb.* 2:14-16).

The second act of the love of Christ towards the elect was that of delight. Christ saw that it was possible for the elect to be redeemed and saved and so his love for them delighted to take up the great work of their salvation to the glory of God.

But why, we may ask, would he who was eternally blessed in his own self-sufficiency be so deeply concerned with our lost, forlorn condition? What moved him to show us compassion and pity? Why did he delight to be our Saviour? Did he see something wonderful in us? No. It was merely the infinite love and goodness of his own nature and not anything in us or of us that moved him to such compassion and pity for us (*Tit.* 3:5).

Christ now being ready and willing to be our mediator, and delighting to take upon himself the work of bringing us back to God, the way by which God planned to restore us was put to him. This way of saving all the elect would involve him in great difficulties and troubles. To the divine nature nothing is too difficult nor is anything too much trouble. But he was to have another nature in which he was to undergo the difficulties of this work of salvation. He was required to pity us until he had none to pity him when he most needed it. He was to tread the way of salvation until his soul was heavy and sorrowful unto death. He was to save us from the wrath and justice of a righteous God by suffering that wrath and justice himself. But far from deterring him, these proposals only heightened his love for us and increased his delight in the work of our salvation. Indeed, his love, like a mighty river, swept over those ominous proposals, for he says, 'Behold, I have come . . . to do your will, O God' (*Heb.* 10:5-7, see also *Isa.* 50:5-7).

So, driven by his eternal love to undertake the office of mediator and the work of our redemption, a body was prepared for him. In this body, or human nature, which he made his own he was to accomplish our salvation. His human nature was filled with immeasurable grace and fervent love to mankind. And by this his human nature was made fit to work out the purpose of eternal love.

From this, it is clear that Christ's glorious love was not only divine but also human. The love of the Father, revealed in his eternal purpose to communicate grace and glory to all the elect was a divine love only. But Christ's love was also human. And in none of those eternal acts of love could the human nature of Christ have any claim or concern. Yet it is the love of the man Christ Jesus which Scripture celebrates.

So that love of Christ for us is the love of his whole person. It is that love which comes from both of his natures, the divine and the human. The acts of love coming from each nature are distinct and different from each other, yet they are all acts of one and the same person. So whether we consider the eternal love of the divine nature or the love of the human nature, revealed here on earth, it is the love of the one and self-same person, Jesus Christ.

It was because of that inexpressible love that the Son of God assumed our nature (*Heb.* 2:14-17). But this act of love was from his divine nature only, because it was before the human nature existed. His laying down his life for us was also an act of inexpressible love (*1 John* 3:6). Yet it was only the love of the human nature in which he offered himself and died. But both these acts of love were acts of his divine-human person. So it is said that God laid down his life for us, and purchased his church with his own blood.

This is that love which makes Christ so glorious, and which we are by faith to behold. A great part of the blessedness of the saints in heaven and their triumph lies in beholding the glory of Christ and what glorious results his work as mediator has produced (see *Rev.* 5:9-10).

What the saints in heaven see of this glory of Christ is beyond our understanding. Here, this love is beyond our knowledge. There, we shall understand all the dimensions of it. Yet even here, if we are not lazy or worldly, we may behold the glory of Christ's love by faith. And where understanding fails, let worship and adoration take place.

So make every effort to prepare your minds for such heavenly thoughts. If your thoughts are filled with earthly things, then a sense of Christ's love and its glory will not abide in them. Few minds are prepared for this duty. The outward behaviour of most reveals the attitude of their souls. Their thoughts wander up and down to the corners of the earth. It is useless to call such persons to the duty of contemplating the glory of Christ's love as mediator. A holy calmness of mind ruled by spiritual principles, a heavenly mindedness, and a realization of how excellent this divine glory is, are required for this duty of meditation.

We must not allow ourselves to be satisfied with vague ideas of the love of Christ which present nothing of his glory to our minds, for it is by such thoughts that many deceive themselves. All who believe that Christ is God value his love and so are never happy with vague ideas of his love as mediator. To have clear, distinct ideas of Christ's love, ask yourself the following questions:

(i) Whose love is it? It is the love of the divine person of the Son of God who laid down his life for us (*1 John* 3:16).

(ii) How did this love of the Son of God show itself? It showed itself in the divine nature by eternal acts of wisdom, goodness and grace. And in the human nature it revealed itself by deeds of pity and compassion, shown by his works and his sufferings for us (*Eph.* 3:19, *Heb.* 2:14-15, *Rev.* 1:5).

(iii) Did we deserve Christ's love? No, we deserved wrath, not love. This thought should be enough to humble you and bring you into the best attitude of mind to meditate on the glory of Christ's love as mediator.

(iv) What did the love of God procure for us? It procured our eternal salvation and our enjoyment of God for ever.

With such clear ideas of the love of Christ, and by worship, you may walk in the paradise of God and enjoy the sweet perfume of his mediatorial love (*Song of Sol.* 2:2-4).

Finally, do not be content to have right ideas of the love of Christ in your mind unless you have a gracious taste of it in your heart. You may taste that the Lord is gracious, that is, you may experience for yourself his grace in your heart. If you do not actually experience the love of Christ in your heart, you will not retain the idea of it in your mind.

Christ is the meat, the bread, the food provided by God

for your soul. And there is no higher spiritual nourishment in Christ than his mediatory love, and this you should always desire. In his love, Christ is glorious. No creatures, angels or men could have the least idea of it before it was revealed by Christ. And after it was seen in this world, it is still absolutely incomprehensible.

6: *The Glory of Christ's Work as Mediator*

As the Lord Christ was glorious in his humbling himself to take up the office of mediator, so also is he glorious in his work as mediator.

An unseen glory accompanied him in all that he did and in all he suffered. It was unseen to the eyes of the world, but not in his eyes who alone judges rightly. Had men seen it they would not have crucified the Lord of glory. Yet some did see this glory (*John* 1:14). But others could see neither 'form nor comeliness and no beauty that he should be desired' (*Isa.* 53:2). It is the same today.

How then did Christ carry out his office as mediator? Man as a creature is subject to the law of God. His duty is to obey God. But there is no true obedience that is done unwillingly. Man could in no way avoid the duty of obedience to God. He is subject to God's law whether he likes it or not.

But with Christ it was not so. He, willingly and of his own choice, subjected himself to the law of God. He obeyed because he willingly chose to obey. Only later, when he assumed human nature, was he obliged to obey. He said, 'Behold, I come to do your will, O God,' before he was obliged to do that will. By his own choice, and that in an act of infinite humility and love, he was 'made of a woman', and thereby 'made under the law'. In his divine person, he was Lord of the law, above the law, in no way liable to its claims or to its curse.

✓ This willingness was the glory of his obedience. This wisdom, grace, love and humility that motivated his choice gave rise to everything he did in obedience to God's will, making it lovely in the sight of God and the means of a righteousness for us. So when he went to John to be baptized, John, knowing he had no need of it because he was sinless, would have refused to administer that ordinance to him. But Jesus replied, 'Permit it to be so now, for thus it is fitting for us to fulfil all righteousness' (*Matt.* 3:15). 'This I have undertaken willingly, of my own free choice, not having any need of it for myself, and therefore I will submit myself to be baptized.' By this submission he revealed his glorious grace as mediator.

✓ His obedience was not for himself but for us. We were obliged to obey and could not. He was not obliged to obey, but by a free act of his own will, did. God gave him this honour, that he should obey for the whole church, so that by 'his obedience many should be made righteous' (*Rom.* 5:19). The reason why I say that God gave him this honour and glory is because his obedience was to stand instead of our obedience in the matter of justification. His obedience, being absolutely perfect, revealed the holiness of God in the law. The ten commandments written on tablets of stone were glorious. But how much more glorious they became when written in the hearts of believers. But only in the holiness and obedience of Christ was this full glory seen. And this obedience is no small part of his glory. Through his human nature the glory of God's holiness was fully revealed by his perfect obedience.

Furthermore, Christ was perfectly obedient in the face of all difficulties and oppositions. Although he had no sin in him to hinder his obedience as we have, yet out-wardly he was confronted with much that would turn him from the path of obedience. Temptations, sufferings, reproaches and contradictions were all hurled at him. So 'though he was a Son, yet he learned obedience by the things which he suffered' (*Heb.* 5:8).

But the glory of his obedience becomes more wonder-ful when we realize who he was who thus obeyed God. He was none other than the Son of God made man. He who was in heaven, above all, Lord of all, lived in the world, having no earthly glory or reputation, obliged to obey the whole law of God perfectly. He, to whom prayer was made, prayed himself night and day. He, whom all the angels of heaven and all creatures worshipped, fulfilled all the duties which the worship of God required. He who was Lord and master of the house became the lowliest servant in the house, performing all menial duties. He that made all men in whose hand they are all as clay is in the hand of the potter, observed among them the strictest rules of jus-tice, in giving to everyone his due, and out of love giving good things to the undeserving. This is what makes the obedience of Christ so mysterious and glorious.

The glory of Christ is also to be seen in his sufferings. 'Ought not the Christ to have suffered these things and to enter into his glory?' asked the risen Lord (*Luke* 24:26). But how can we begin to think of the sufferings of Christ?

We might see him under the weight of God's wrath and the curse of the law, taking upon himself and on his whole soul the utmost that God had ever threatened to sin or sin-ners. We might see him in his agony and bloody sweat, in his strong cries and supplications, when he was sorrowful unto death and filled with horror at the sight of those things which were coming upon him, the dreadful trial he was about to enter. We might see him wrestling with all the powers of darkness, the rage and madness of men, and suffering all this in his soul, his body, his name, his reputation, his goods and his life. Some of these sufferings were inflicted directly by God, others came from devils and wicked men, acting according to the determinate counsel of God. We might see him praying, weeping, crying out, bleeding, dying, making his soul an offering for sin (*Isa.* 53:8).

Lord, what is man that you are so mindful of him? And the son of man that you visit him? Who has known your mind, or who has been your counsellor? O the depths of the riches both of the wisdom and the knowledge of God! How unsearchable are his judgements, and his ways past finding out! What shall we say to these things? That God did not spare his Son, but gave him up to death, and all the sufferings associated with that death, for such poor lost sinners! That for our sakes the eternal Son of God should submit himself to all that our sinful natures were liable to, and our sins deserved, that we might be delivered!

How glorious the Lord Jesus Christ is in the eyes of believers! When Adam sinned, he stood ashamed, afraid, trembling, as one ready to perish for ever under the severe displeasure of God. Death was what he deserved, and he fully expected the sentence to be immediately carried out. In this state, the Lord Christ in the promise comes to him, and says, 'Poor creature! How terrible is your condition! How deformed you are now! What has become of the beauty, the glory of that image of God in which you were created? See how you have taken upon yourself the monstrous shape and image of Satan? And yet your present sorrow, your physical return to dust and darkness, is in no way to be compared with what is to follow. Eternal distress lies before you. But now, look up and behold me, and you will have a glimpse of what infinite wisdom, love and grace have purposed for you. Do not continue to hide from me. I will take your place. I will bear your guilt and suffer that punishment which would sink you eternally into the hideous depths of hell. I will pay for what I never took. I will be made a curse for you so that you may be eternally blessed.' In the same vein the Lord Christ speaks to all convicted sinners when he invites them to come to him.

This is how the Lord Christ is presented in the gospel as 'evidently crucified' before our eyes (*Gal.* 3:1). This is how the glory of his sufferings shines forth.

Let us, then, consider him as poor, despised, persecuted, reproached, reviled, crucified, suffering the wrath of God due to our sins. These things are recorded in the gospel for us to read, to preach and to consider in the duty of meditation.

But what can we see of his sufferings in the gospel? What glory do we see in these things? Are not these the things at which both Jews and Gentiles stumbled and which they found offensive? Was it not thought to be foolish to look for salvation by the sorrows and miseries of another, to look for life by his death? Paul tells us that it was (see *1 Cor.* 1:18-25). The wisdom of the world despised the sufferings of Christ. But it is precisely because of his sufferings that he is glorious and precious in the sight of

[61]

believers (*1 Pet.* 2:6-7). For in these sufferings Christ was 'the power of God and the wisdom of God' (*1 Cor.* 1:24). It is only because the god of this world has blinded their eyes that men fail to see the meaning of the cross of Christ (*2 Cor.* 4:3-6). But it is in these sufferings that we behold the glory of Christ's work as mediator.

7: *The Glory of Christ's Exaltation*

All the prophecies and predictions concerning Jesus Christ under the Old Testament can be classified under two headings, namely, his sufferings and the glory that would follow (*1 Pet.* 1:11). So when Christ opened the Scriptures to his disciples, he said, 'Ought not the Christ to have suffered these things and to enter into His glory?' (*Luke* 24:26, see also *Rom.* 14:9, *Phil.* 2:5-9). Only as we understand his sufferings and glory do we really grasp the message of Scripture.

So the mediatory work of Christ involved both suffering and glory. And so he calls his church to follow him, first through sufferings and then into glory. 'If we suffer, we shall also reign with him' (*2 Tim.* 2:12). Some would reign now on this earth, and we may say with Paul, 'Would you did reign, that we might reign with you.' But the members of the mystical body must be conformed to the Head. In Christ, sufferings went before glory. And so it must be with us. Satan and the world both offer immediate glory, but this glory will be followed by eternal suffering. First the good things of this life, and then eternal misery is the way of this world and its god (*Luke* 16:25).

Suffering and glory are the two anointed ones that stand before the Lord of the whole earth, from which all the golden oil, by which the church is dedicated to God and sanctified, flows. The glory of Christ in the exaltation into which he entered after his sufferings is what we are now going to see.

Christ prayed that his disciples might be where he now is in order to see the glory of his exaltation. While he was in the world a veil was drawn over this glory. But now, in his state of exaltation, the veil is removed and the glory of his purpose and his mediatory work is now revealed. This is the glory which the Father gave him before the foundation of the world, and with which he was actually invested when he ascended into heaven. When we see *this* glory, we shall see Christ as he really is.

The 'glory of Christ' is not the essential glory of his divine nature, but the revelation of the glory after it had been veiled in this world under the 'form of a servant'. The divine glory itself does not belong to Christ's exaltation. But the *revelation* of his divine glory does belong to his exaltation. He was not *made* God as a free gift when he was exalted, but *declared to be* God to the church of angels and men after his state of humiliation. He did not discard his divine glory while in the world, but the direct sight of this divine glory he laid aside, until he was 'declared to be the Son of God with power' by the resurrection from the dead.

A total eclipse of the sun does not destroy its natural beauty, light and glory. It is still the same as it was in the beginning, 'a great light to rule the day'. So the glory of Christ in his divine nature was deliberately eclipsed in his state of humiliation on the earth. But now the glory of his divine nature shines forth in its infinite lustre. And when those who saw him on earth as a poor, sorrowful, persecuted man, dying on the cross, came to see him in all the infinite, uncreated glories of the divine nature, their souls were filled with transcendent joy and wonder. This is one reason why he prayed for them while he was on earth that they might be with him where he is to behold his glory. He knew it would fully satisfy them for evermore.

Nor is the glory of Christ the glorification of his human nature, though this is included. This is indeed a subject fit for us to think about especially as it shows us that glorified human nature to which he will bring all believers. But because we mean more than this, I shall mention only two things concerning the glorification of his human nature.

That very nature itself which Christ took on him in this world is exalted into glory. Some deny that he has either flesh or blood in heaven, even though they are changed, purified and glorified. The great foundation of the church and all gospel faith is that he was made flesh, he partook of flesh and blood. It would be a heresy to say that he has now forsaken that flesh and blood with which he was made in the womb of the blessed virgin, in which he lived and died, which he offered to God in sacrifice, and in which he rose from the dead.

Of course, we cannot fully understand the true nature of the glorification of the humanity of Christ. But then, it does not yet appear what *we* shall be. Much less is it clear to us what he shall be like. But that he is still in the human nature he had on earth, that he has the same rational soul and the same body, is a fundamental article of the Christian faith.

This nature of the man Christ Jesus is filled with all the divine graces and perfections of which limited, created nature is capable. His human nature was not deified. He was not made a god. He does not in heaven become one with the divine. His human nature has no essential property of deity communicated to it, and is not made omniscient, omnipresent or omnipotent. But it is exalted in a fullness of all divine perfection far above the glory of angels and men. It is incomprehensibly nearer God and has communications from God, in glorious light, love and power far above all angels and men. But it is still a creature.

Believers also shall have a glorified human nature; when we see him as he is, we shall be like him. But our glorified human nature will not be as glorious as his. 'There is one glory of the sun, another glory of the moon, and another glory of the stars; for one star differs from another star in glory' (*1 Cor.* 15:41).

There is a difference in glory among the stars; a greater one between the sun and the stars. Such will be the difference in eternity between the glorified human nature of Christ and the glorified human nature of believers. Nevertheless this is not the true glory of Christ in his exaltation. In what, then, does it consist? The glory of Christ in his exaltation lies in the following:

(i) The exaltation of his human nature in union with the divine nature far above the whole creation in power, dignity, authority and rule, with everything else that the wisdom of God has appointed to make the person of Christ glorious.

(ii) The glory of Christ in his exaltation lies in the infinite love that God the Father has for him, and in the Father's delight and satisfaction in him because of the way he carried out all that he was sent to do. So he is said 'to sit at the right hand of God', or at 'the right hand of the Majesty on high'.

(iii) The glory of Christ in his exaltation is made more wonderful by the full revelation of his own divine wisdom, love and grace in his mediatory work and redemption of the church. Here on earth we see this only by faith; but in heaven it shines forth in all its brightness, to the eternal joy of those who behold him.

This is that glory which our Lord Jesus Christ specially prayed that his disciples might see. This is what by faith we ought to make every effort to consider. By faith and not by imagination!

Proud and foolish men, who have vague ideas of the glory of Christ but know nothing of the real nature of that glory, have tried to present it in images and pictures. This is how the Roman Catholic Church presents the glory of Christ to the imaginations and unspiritual hearts of super-stitious people. But they err, not knowing the Scripture, nor the eternal glory of the Son of God.

The glory of Christ's exaltation cannot be seen or understood in this world except by faith fixing itself on divine revelation. We cannot behold the glory of Christ by conjuring up pictures of him in the mind and by trying to form the shape of a person in heaven in our imag-inations. The way to behold the glory of Christ is by the steady exercise of faith on the revelation of this glory of Christ given to us in Scripture. It is our duty, therefore, constantly to meditate on the glory of Christ. This will fill us with a joy which will, in turn, move us to meditate on his glory more and more.

We are so selfish that we tend not to look any further than our own concerns and interests. So long as we are pardoned and saved we care little about Christ's interests and concerns. But this attitude is not born of a true faith in and love for God. The chief duty of faith and love is to lead us to prefer Christ above ourselves, and his concerns above our own. So let us stir ourselves up to meditate on him by asking ourselves the following questions.

Who is he that is exalted above all? Who is he who has been surrounded with glory, majesty and power? Who is he who is seated at the right hand of the Majesty on high, all his enemies being made his footstool? Is it not he who while in this world was poor, despised, persecuted and slain for us? Is it not the same Jesus who loved us and gave himself for us and washed us from our sin in his own blood? If we value his love, if we realize what he has done and suffered for the church, we cannot but rejoice in his present state and glory.

Blessed Jesus! we can add nothing to you, nothing to your glory. But it is a joy to us that you are what you are— that you are so gloriously exalted at the right hand of God. We long to behold that glory more and more according to your prayer and promise. Amen.

8: *The Glory of Christ under the Old Testament*

Moses and the prophets and all the Scriptures testify to Christ and his glory (*Luke* 24:27). Not to see Christ and his glory in all the Scriptures is to be like the Jews. They had a veil on their minds. Faith alone can remove that veil of darkness which prevents the minds of men from beholding the glory of Christ in the Old Testament (*2 Cor.* 3:14-16). I shall therefore show briefly some of the ways by which the glory of Christ was presented to believers under the Old Testament.

(i)   The glory of Christ under the Old Testament was revealed in the beautiful worship of the law. Why did God command his people to set up a tabernacle and temple? What was the meaning of the holy place with all its utensils? Why were the ten commandments, the ark, the cherubim and the mercy-seat placed in it? What did the high priest clothed in his magnificent vestments teach? Why were sacrifices instituted and why was there an annual sprinkling of blood in the most holy place? What was the meaning of this whole religious worship? Did they not all in one way or another represent Christ in the glory of his person and office? They were a shadow of the real person and glory of Christ.

Everything Moses did in erecting the tabernacle and instituting all its services was intended to testify to the person and glory of Christ which would later be revealed (*Heb.* 3:5). That was the substance of the ministry of the prophets as well (*1 Pet.* 1:11-12).

(ii) The glory of Christ under the Old Testament was represented in the mystical account which is given to us of his communion with his church in love and grace. This is specially seen in the Song of Solomon. King Solomon was a type of Christ, and an instrument of the Holy Spirit in writing Scripture. The Song of Solomon is a gracious record of the divine love and grace of Christ to his church with expressions of her love to and delight in him. The more we have experienced communion with Christ the more we shall appreciate this book and the more it will give light and life to our minds and powerfully communicate to us the power of Christ's love and grace. But because these things are little understood, this book is greatly neglected, if not despised. Indeed, some have wickedly ridiculed its expressions. But we were warned of such mockers in the last days.

The institutions of outward worship and the record of the inward communion Old Testament believers had with Christ in grace, hope and love, give us the substance of that view saints under the Old Testament had of his glory. And if we who have received far greater revelations of the same glory do not show a far greater desire to behold the glory of Christ, we shall one day be judged unworthy to have received him.

(iii) The glory of Christ was represented and made known under the Old Testament in his personal appearances to leaders of the church in their generations. In these appearances he was God only, but appeared in the assumed shape of a man, to signify what he would one day actually be. He did not create a human nature and unite it to himself for a while. Rather, by his divine power he appeared in the shape of a man. In this way, Christ appeared to Abraham, to Jacob, to Moses, to Joshua and to others.

Furthermore, because Christ was the divine person who dwelt in and with the church under the Old Testament, he constantly assumed human feelings and emotions, to intimate that a time would come when he would assume human nature. In fact, after the fall everything said of God in the Old Testament ultimately refers to the future incarnation of Christ. It would have been absurd to represent God as grieving, repenting, being angry and well-pleased and exhibiting all other human emotions, were it not that the divine person intended to take on him human nature in which such emotions dwell.

(iv) The glory of Christ under the Old Testament was represented in prophetic visions. So John tells us Isaiah's vision of the glory of the Lord was a vision of the glory of Christ (*Isa.* 6; *John* 12:41). 'The train of his robe filled the temple' (*Isa.* 6:1). This symbolized the glorious grace which filled the temple of his body. This is the true tabernacle, which God pitched, and not man; it is the temple which was destroyed, and which he raised again in three days, in which dwelt the fullness of the Godhead (*Col.* 2:9). This glory was revealed to Isaiah, and it filled him with fear and astonishment. But by the ministry of one of the glorious seraphim, his iniquity was taken away by a coal from the altar, which symbolized the sacrificial blood which cleanses from all sin. This is food indeed for the souls of believers.

Of the same nature was his glorious appearance on

Mount Sinai at the giving of the law (*Exod.* 19). This is described by the psalmist and applied by Paul to the ascension of Christ following his resurrection (*Ps.* 68:17-18, *Eph.* 4:8). There was much to terrify the people when the law was given because of its holiness and the severity of the curse. Yet the psalmist refers to the giving of the law as full of mercy in reference to Christ's fulfilling perfectly all the demands of the same law. His giving of the law was as death to them because of its righteousness and curse. His fulfilling of the law brought life because it procured pardon and righteousness which he gives freely to his people.

(v) The doctrine of Christ's incarnation was revealed under the Old Testament although not as clearly as it is revealed in the gospel. One instance will suffice. 'For unto us a child is born, unto us a Son is given; and the government will be upon his shoulder. And his name will be called Wonderful, Counsellor, Mighty God, Everlasting Father, Prince of Peace. Of the increase of his government and peace there will be no end' (*Isa.* 9:6-7). This one testimony is sufficient to confound all Jews and other enemies of the glory of Christ. I admit that, notwithstanding this revelation, there remained much darkness in the minds of those to whom the revelation was then made. Although they did accept the truth of the revelation, yet they could have no idea how it would be accomplished. But now, when every word of it is explained and declared and its mystical meaning laid open to us in the incarnation itself which fulfilled in every way the Scripture predictions, it is blindness not to receive it. Nothing but our satanic pride, which will not accept what we cannot understand, makes us shut our eyes against the light of this truth.

(vi) The glory of Christ under the Old Testament was revealed in promises, prophecies and predictions about his person, his coming, his offices, his kingdom and his glory. With the wisdom, grace and love of God to the church, these things are the lifeline running through all the writings of the Old Testament and take up a great part of them. These were the things which Christ expounded to his disciples out of Moses and all the prophets. Concerning these things, Christ appealed to the Scriptures against his opponents, saying, 'Search the Scriptures, for they are they which testify of me.' If we do not see the glory of Christ in the Scriptures it is because a veil of blindness is over our minds. Nor can we read, study or become spiritually strong by meditating on the writings of the Old Testament unless we commit ourselves to considering the glory of Christ displayed in them. So to many the Bible is a sealed book.

(vii) The glory of Christ under the Old Testament is revealed under many metaphorical expressions. So Christ is called the rose, for the sweet perfume of his love, grace and obedience. He is called the lily for the beauty of his grace and love. In the New Testament he is called the pearl of great price because he is precious to believers. He is called the vine for his fruitfulness. He is called the lamb for his meekness and fitness for his sacrifice.

From all of this let us learn to behold the glory of Christ when we read the Old Testament Scriptures.

9: *The Glory of Christ's Union with the Church*

There is an intimate union between Christ and his church. This makes it just and right in the sight of God that what Christ did and suffered should be reckoned and imputed to us as if we had done and suffered the same things ourselves. This union took place by his choice, and because of it believers see him as glorious indeed.

Peter tells us that 'in his own self [Christ] bore our sins in his own body on the tree' (*1 Pet.* 2:24). He 'suffered once for sins, the just for the unjust, that he might bring us to God' (*1 Pet.* 3:18). But reason cannot accept this. 'Where is the justice of it?' it asks. 'It isn't fair that the just should suffer for the unjust. Where is divine righteousness to be seen in this?' But Scripture replies: 'The Lord has laid on him the iniquity of us all' (*Isa.* 53:6).

How is it that this was just and fair?

First, it is certain that all the elect, the whole church of God, fell in Adam under the curse due to the transgression of the law. By this curse, death, both physical and eternal is meant. This curse no man could undergo and be saved. Nor was it consistent with the righteousness of God that sin should go unpunished. So it was necessary, since God had purposed to save his church, to transfer the punishment from them who deserved it but could not bear it, to one who had not deserved it but could bear it. This transfer of punishment by divine dispensation is the foundation of the Christian faith, indeed of all the supernatural revelation contained in Scripture.

Second, it was suggested in the first promise, and later explained and confirmed in all the institutions of the Old Testament. In the sacrifices of the law there was a revival of the greatest and most fundamental principle of the law of nature, namely, that God is to be worshipped with our best. But their chief function was to represent this transfer of punishment from the offender to another, who was to be a sacrifice instead of the sinner.

This is just, righteous and fair for the following reasons:

(i) This transfer of punishment is not contrary to divine justice. It does not interfere with the law of nature that in many cases some persons should suffer punishment for the sins and offences of others. The Bible gives many examples.

God says he will do exactly this in Exodus 20:5: 'Visiting the iniquity of the fathers on the children to the third and fourth generations of those who hate Me'. It does not matter that the children are also sinners, following in their fathers' sins, for the worst of sinners must not have any injustice done to him. But the children must have had the fathers' sins transferred to them if they are punished for their fathers' sins. Therefore it is not unlawful for anyone to be punished for the sins of another. In the Babylonian captivity, the sins of the fathers—especially the sins of Manasseh—were visited on the children (*Lam.* 5:7, *2 Kings* 23:26-27, see also *Luke* 11:50-51).

Again, Canaan was cursed for the sin of his father (*Gen.* 9:25). Saul's seven sons were put to death for their father's murderous cruelty (*2 Sam.* 21:9-14). For the sin of David, seventy thousand were destroyed: 'Surely I have sinned, and I have done wickedly, but these sheep, what have they done?' he said (*2 Sam.* 24:15-17). So it was with all the children and infants that perished in the destruction of both Sodom and Gomorrah.

There is no injustice in God, so the transfer of the sins of some to others who are punished for them must be just and fair.

Divine justice does not arbitrarily punish someone for the sins of others. There is always a special reason why the sins of some are transferred to others: there must be a special union or relationship between those who sin and those who are punished for their sins. Before the punishment of sin can be transferred to another there must be a special relationship or union between the two persons. We can take as examples, the relationship between parents and children, and also a king and his subjects, as in the case of David. The persons sinning and those suffering for their sins are treated as one body, in which when one member sins another member of the same body may justly suffer for that sin. The backside may be punished for what the hand has stolen or the mouth has spoken.

Before the punishment of sin can be transferred from one to another, those involved must have a mutual interest or concern. A biblical example is seen in Numbers 14:32-33. Both the fathers and the children were concerned to get into the promised land. But the fathers' faithlessness led to both fathers and children having to wander forty years in the wilderness.

(ii) There is a greater, more wonderful union between Christ and his church which makes it just and fair in the sight of God that Christ should suffer for us, and that what he did and suffered should be imputed or transferred to us. This I now intend to clarify.

There are and can be only three sorts of union between separate persons who are quite different from each other.

(a)   The first union is a natural union. God has made all mankind 'of one blood' (*Acts* 17:26). So every man is every other man's brother or neighbour to whom care, love and kindness must be shown (*Luke* 10:36). This union also exists between Christ and his church (*Heb.* 2:14-15).

So 'he who sanctifies and those who are being sanctified are all of one' (*Heb.* 2:11). His infinite willingness to humble himself in coming into this communion and union of nature with us we have clearly seen. But this union is quite different from that of all other men who have the same nature.

The union between Christ and his church did not arise by necessity of nature, but from a voluntary act of his will. All other unions are necessary. Every man is every man's brother whether he likes it or not, because the union is by natural generation. But this was not so with Christ. He came into this natural union with us of his own free choice, because the children were already partakers of flesh and blood. He would be what the children were. So the union of Christ in human nature with the church is gloriously different from that union which is amongst all others in the same nature. And therefore, although it may not be considered right among mere men that one should suffer for others, because their union with each other is forced upon them and not by their free choice, yet with the Lord Christ it is quite different. The union he has with the church was by his own free choice.

Christ voluntarily entered into this union for the special purpose that he might do and suffer what was to be done and suffered by the church. So the writer to the Hebrews says, 'That through death he might destroy him who had the power of death, that is, the devil, and release those who through fear of death were all their lifetime subject to bondage' (*Heb*. 2:14-15). This was the reason for his union with the church. Christ willingly chose to take the punishment of death for the sins of his church, and for that reason took into union with himself their nature. And in this union he is glorious and precious to believers.

(b)   There is a mystical union between Christ and the church which corresponds to all the most strict, real or moral unions between other persons or things. Such is the union between the head of a body and its members, or the vine and its branches which is real, or between a husband and wife which is moral and real also (see *Eph*. 5:25-32).

As the head and husband of the church Christ became responsible for all the debts incurred by his wife. He was to sanctify and save her and she could not be saved but by his sufferings and the shedding of his blood on the cross. But because he was the church's head and husband, it was appropriate for him to suffer in her place and it was righteous also that what he did and suffered should be imputed to each and every member of the church for whom he suffered. The glory of Christ in this union is unique. As such it is seen by those who in some measure understand this mystery.

Objection

This mystical union of Christ with his church was only

after he suffered for her, for it follows the conversion of men to him. It is *by faith* that we are united to him. Until that union with him has been wrought in us we have no mystical union with him. He is not a head or husband to unregenerate, unsanctified unbelievers. But such was the state of the whole church when Christ suffered for us (*Rom.* 5:8; *Eph.* 2:5). There was, therefore, no such mystical union between Christ and the church that made it just and right that he should suffer instead of them. So the church is the result of the work of redemption and as such it could not have been redeemed by virtue of a union that existed before the work of salvation.

Answer

Although this mystical union does not actually take place until believers are united to Christ, yet the church of the elect was chosen to be Christ's spouse before his sufferings, in order that he might love her and suffer for her. We have here the example of Jacob who served Laban many years for a wife (*Hos.* 12:12). Nevertheless Rachel did not become his wife until after he had served for her, and by his service he purchased her to be his wife. Yet, while he is serving for her, she is called his wife, because of his love for her, and because she was going to be his wife when he had completed his service for her. So the church was to be the spouse of Christ in God's purpose, and so Christ loved her and gave himself for her.

So in the work of redemption, it was the church which was to be redeemed because she was to be the spouse of Christ. And the result of that redemption was that it made possible the actual union between Christ and his church.

Behind all that Christ did and suffered for the church,

there was a supreme act of the will of God the Father, giving all the elect to him, entrusting them to him, to be redeemed, sanctified and saved (*John* 17:6, 9, 10, 14-16).

On these grounds this mystical union between Christ and his church was real before it actually came into being.

(c) There is also a federal union, a union formed by a treaty, a contract or a covenant drawn up between the persons concerned. So the Lord Christ undertook to be the surety of the new covenant on behalf of the church (*Heb.* 7:22). So as surety he gave himself to God to fulfil all the demands of God's law and justice on behalf of the church so that they might be sanctified and saved. So by reason of this union it was just and right for God to impute our sins to Christ and his obedience and death to us, treating us as if we had obeyed and died for our own sins. So it is in this union that Christ is exceedingly glorious and precious to believers. No heart can conceive or tongue express the glory of Christ in this union.

This union of Christ and his church shines forth in the exaltation of the righteousness of God in the forgiveness of sins. By virtue of his union with his church into which he freely and willingly entered, it was an act of God's righteous justice to lay all the punishment of our sins on him so that he might graciously pardon them all to the honour and glory of his justice as well as of his grace and mercy (*Rom.* 3:24-26).

Because of this union Christ is glorious in the sight of God, angels and men. In Christ both the justice and mercy of God are glorified. By his cross, divine holiness and justice were exalted, and through his triumph, grace and mercy are poured out to the full. In glorious thoughts of this let my soul live, and in believing it let my soul die. And let the present wonder of this glory make way for the eternal enjoyment of it in its beauty and fullness.

Christ is glorious in that perfect obedience to the law of God on behalf of his church. This obedience was absolutely necessary to exalt the wisdom, holiness and righteousness of God in giving the law. When man fell he could no longer keep the law. But through the obedience of Christ, by virtue of his mystical union with the church, the law was perfectly obeyed in us by being obeyed for us. Now the glory of God in giving the law and its promised rewards is seen in all its perfection (see *Rom.* 8:3-4).

One view of Christ's glory by faith will scatter all the fears, answer all the objections and disperse all the depressions of poor, tempted, doubting souls. To all believers it is an anchor which they may cast within the veil, to hold them firm and steadfast in all trials, storms and temptations, both in life and in death.

10: *The Glory of Christ's Giving Himself to Believers*

Another element in the glory of Christ which we ought to consider here by faith and look forward to seeing hereafter, lies in the mysterious giving of himself and all the blessings of his mediatory work to the souls of believers for their present happiness and their eternal blessedness. By this mysterious communication of himself to believers, he becomes theirs as they are his. This is the life, glory and comfort of the church (*Song of Sol.* 6:3; 2:17; 7:10).

Paul, speaking of Christ's communication of himself to the church and the union between them says that it is 'a great mystery', for 'I speak', he says, 'concerning Christ and the church' (*Eph.* 5:32).

We need to learn how he communicates himself to us; how he is made to be ours, to be in us, to dwell with us and to impart all the blessings of his mediatory work to us.

Christ does not communicate himself to us because he must, as the sun must give light to all the world. Nor is he present with everyone because of his omnipresence, nor, as some dream, by a diffusion of his soul into all. Nor does he become ours by a physical eating of the bread in the sacrament as Roman Catholics imagine.

But before we consider how he communicates himself to us, it will be helpful first to say something about divine communications and the glory of them in general.

The first thing we need to know about divine communications is that all life, power, goodness and wisdom are in God essentially and infinitely, and come to us only from him.

God created all things by his almighty power, guided and directed by his infinite wisdom and goodness. To all creation he communicated his goodness and to his living creatures he communicated life as well as goodness. This was the first of God's communications to his creation. It was exceedingly glorious (see *Ps.* 19:1, *Rom.* 1:20). God created all things in such a way that they are dependent on each other. The earth, for example, depends on the sun and the rain for all that it produces (see *Hos.* 2:21-22). In this mutual dependence all things depend on and are influenced by God himself, the eternal source of being, power and goodness (*Acts* 14:15-17; 17:24-29).

The glory of God is thus obvious to the human mind, for by his works and providence his eternal power and Godhead are revealed.

But by this divine communication God did not mean only to glorify his divine nature but also his eternal existence in three persons, Father, Son and Spirit.

The whole creation in all its perfection came forth from the power and goodness of the divine nature, from the Father who is said to be the Creator of all things. Yet the actual work of creation was committed to the Son, the power and wisdom of the Father (*John* 1:1-3, *Col.* 1:16, *Heb.* 1:2). But it was the Holy Spirit who, when the first mass of creation was produced, hovered over it as a bird over its eggs, keeping it and cherishing it so that it was able to produce all kinds of creatures (*Gen.* 1:2). So, in the maintenance of the whole, there is a special work of the Holy Spirit in all things. Nothing can continue to exist for one moment except by the power of the Holy Spirit (*Ps.* 104:29-30).

By these divine communications in producing and preserving the creation, God reveals his glory. Without them, he would still have been for ever essentially glorious, but it would have been impossible for his glory to have been known by anyone but himself. So it is on these divine communications that the revelation of his glory depends. And as we shall see, the revelation of his glory is even far more wonderful in the new creation.

All goodness, grace, life, light, mercy and power which are the cause of the new creation come from God, from his divine nature. Because of them God is eternally or essentially glorious in himself, and the purpose of the new creation was to reveal the glory of these characteristics by their being communicated to those in the new creation. By the church, the true, glorious character of God was to be seen and known.

The first communication of these things was made to Christ as the head of the church (*Col.* 1:17-19). Christ was the repository and treasury of all the goodness, grace, life, light, power and mercy which were necessary to set up and preserve the church. They were to dwell in him and to be communicated from him to the whole mystical body of the church. This communication to Christ was first to his person. It is in his person that all fullness dwells (*Col.* 2:3, 9, *Eph.* 3:8-11). Then, by means of his mediatory office as prophet, priest and king, the things communicated to him were to be communicated by him to the church.

The decree of election prepared, as it were, the material for the production of the church, the new creation

In the creation of the world, God first created and prepared the matter, which, by the power of the Holy Spirit was formed into all the different and various creatures. He gave life to them according to their distinct kinds.

Similarly, in producing and perfecting the work of the church from eternity, in the holy purpose of his will, God prepared and set apart for himself those he had chosen for salvation. They were the special matter that was to be worked on by the Holy Spirit in the production of the glorious fabric of the church. Thus what was said by the psalmist about the natural body of man may also be said of the mystical body of Christ (see *Ps.* 139:15-16).

So from the infinite, eternal spring of wisdom, grace, goodness and love in the Father came the decree of election. Those whom God chose out of this sinful human race for the new creation, he entrusted to Christ. He appointed him their Saviour, to bring them out of the old creation which was cursed into the new. By the power of the Holy Spirit he planned to apply all the blessings of the salvation wrought by Christ and thus communicate life, light, power, grace and mercy to all the elect. In doing this God glorifies both the essential properties of his nature, his infinite wisdom, power, goodness and grace and also his glorious existence in three persons. The glorious truth of the Trinity is thus made precious to believers and becomes the foundation of their faith and hope. When we understand and meditate on the glorious way by which God communicates his divine properties to us by the Son and the Spirit, we see the glory of his nature in the three distinct persons of the Father, Son and Holy Spirit.

According to this divine order, the elect in all ages are,

by the Holy Spirit working on them, brought to spiritual life, light, grace and power to the glory of God. They are not called by chance. In every age, at his own time, the Holy Spirit communicates these things to them to the glory of each person in the holy Trinity.

In the same way the whole new creation is kept from ever falling away again. Every moment, power, strength, mercy and grace are communicated from the Father through the Son by the Holy Spirit. There is a continual outflow of graces from the Head to all members of the body working in them both to will and to do of his own good pleasure. Paul declares that the whole church order is organized to promote these divine communications to all the members of the church itself (*Eph.* 4:13-15).

This is how divine graces are communicated to the church even in heaven throughout eternity. But at present, the world can neither see this nor understand it, so it despises it because it sees no glory in it. But let us make Paul's prayer for spiritual understanding of these things ours (*Eph.* 1:16-23). For the revelation of God's glory in the old creation is very inferior to that which he makes of himself in the new.

Having seen in general the glory of God's way of communicating himself, we must now consider how Christ communicates himself and the blessings arising from his mediatory work to believers.

Christ becomes ours as a free gift from the Father (*1 Cor.* 1:30, *Rom.* 5:15-17). This act of the Father in giving us his Son arises from his eternal purpose to glorify his grace in his elect by giving Christ and all the blessings of his mediatory work to them (*Eph.* 1:3-14).

God also gave all the elect to Christ and this he did before Christ was offered freely to them. 'They were yours and you gave them to me' (*John* 17:6).

This gift of Christ was, in turn, promised in the gospel, so that all who receive him or believe in him become partakers of the blessings that he has procured for them (*John* 1:12, *1 John* 1:1-4). To enable his elect to receive Christ God creates faith in the souls of all the elect by his almighty power (*Eph.* 1:19-20; 2:5-8).

This wonderful gift of Christ to the church arises out of the eternal counsel, wisdom, grace and power of the Father. But what we are interested in is *how* Christ gives himself, because this reveals the glory of his wisdom, love and humility.

In order to give himself to us, Christ gives us the Holy Spirit. The Holy Spirit was given to him to live in him in all his fullness by the Father. This Spirit, dwelling in Christ in all his fullness, Christ in turn gives to all believers to dwell in them (*John* 14:14-20, *1 Cor.* 6:17, *Rom.* 8:9). Thus the glorious union between Christ and believers is brought about. For as in his incarnation he took our nature into personal union with his own, so by the Holy Spirit he takes us into a mystical union with himself.

This mystical union is a glorious illustration of God's wisdom. The same Spirit who dwells in him as the head dwells in the church as his body, giving life to all the elect.

There is no parallel to this in all creation. Natural unions and relationships, such as marriage, are but shadows of it (*Eph.* 5:25-32). So in this union the Lord Christ is precious to believers. But at the same time he is a stone of stumbling and rock of offence to the disobedient. For many people despise this work of wisdom and grace. They know what it means to be joined to one's marriage partner so as to become one flesh, but they have no idea what it is to be joined to the Lord so as to become one spirit. By this union with Christ the spiritual life of the church and of all the church's ability to respond to God and to heavenly things is secured. By this union 'our life is hid with Christ in God'; the glory, honour and security of the church are eternally preserved, to the praise of God's grace. So to understand Christ's union with the church and the communication of himself to his people is more desirable than to understand all the wisdom in the world.

Christ communicates himself to us by creating a new nature, his own nature, in us. The very same spiritual nature which is in him is also in the church, but with this difference: in Christ all graces reside in absolute perfection, whereas in us graces exist in various measures as he is pleased to communicate them to us. But it is still the same divine nature in him as in us, for through the precious promises of the gospel we are made partakers of the divine nature. It is not enough that he should take our nature upon him, unless he gives his nature to be ours. He implants in our souls all those graces which were in his human nature. This is that new man, the new creature, that divine nature, that spirit which is born of the Spirit, that transformation into the image of Christ, that putting on of Christ, that workmanship created in us by God for good works, that Scripture describes (*John* 3:6, *Rom.* 6:3-8, *2 Cor.* 3:18; 5:17, *Eph.* 4:20-24, *2 Pet.* 1:4).

This new, heavenly nature which is formed in believers as the first vital act of their union with Christ by the indwelling of the same Spirit is unique to his nature. We are predestined to be conformed to his image and it is this image that is produced in our souls by the power and virtue which come from Christ. Thus 'of God are we in Christ Jesus, who became for us wisdom from God—and righteousness and sanctification and redemption'. So Christ says of his church, 'This is now bone of my bones, and flesh of my flesh. I see myself, my own nature in them, so to me they are beautiful and desirable.'

By thus communicating his nature to his church Christ is able to 'present it to himself a glorious church, not having spot or wrinkle or any such thing, but holy and without blemish'. All the purity, the beauty, the holiness and the inward glory of the church depend on this. The church is thus in every way separated from the world, and differs from all others who outwardly appear to be very religious and seem to be the same as true Christians.

By this communication of Christ to us, the church becomes the first-fruits of creation to God, bearing anew God's image in the world. In all these things Christ is and will be glorious to all eternity.

Christ unites himself to us by engrafting us into himself by faith (which is his own work wrought in us). By this engrafting he communicates himself to us. He does this by the grace or power of the gospel, and by the law or requirements of the gospel, both of which have a great influence in this mystical communication of Christ to the church.

By the grace and power of the gospel we continually receive perpetual supplies of spiritual life, support, strength, grace and perseverance. This is what he teaches us in the parable of the vine and its branches (*John* 15:1-5). They live, nevertheless not they, but Christ lives in them, and the life which they lead in the flesh is by the faith of the Son of God (*Gal.* 2:20). By virtue of the law and requirements of the gospel, Christ's righteousness and all the fruits of his mediatory work are imputed to us. The glory of this mystery is opened to us by St Paul in Romans chapters three to five.

There are also other ways by which we experience our union with Christ. His love is shed abroad in our hearts by the Holy Spirit who is given to us. and we are enabled to love Christ in return by the almighty work of the same Spirit. There is indeed a deep mystery and glory in this loving relationship.

We would also mention his work as prophet, priest and king and all the blessings we have from him in these offices. But the few examples that have been given of the glory of Christ in this mysterious communication of himself to his church are sufficient to give us such a sight of it as to fill our hearts with holy wonder and gratitude.

11: *The Glory of Christ in Restoring All Things*

Sin has caused devastation in the world. It has brought disharmony and disunity to the nations in the world. But God in his wisdom and sovereign pleasure has appointed his Son, Jesus Christ, as the means of restoring all things. It is his work to bring all things into unity and harmony in himself.

Paul describes this gathering together in one all things in Christ in his letter to the Ephesians (*Eph.* 1:18-20). Several things must be made clear if we are to understand this.

The first is that God has all existence in himself. He calls himself 'I AM' (*Exod.* 3:14). In him all things existed potentially before they existed actually. So all things are 'of him, and through him and to him' (*Rom.* 11:36). Moreover his own existence is goodness itself. In his goodness God communicates the effects of his goodness to us. So the first thing we learn about God is that his infinite Being and goodness exist together in a nature which is both intelligent and self-existent (see *Heb.* 11:6).

In this state of infinite, eternal Being and goodness, before he had called anything into existence by his wisdom or power, God was eternally in himself all that he will be and all that he can be, for ever and ever. For where there is infinite Being and infinite goodness, there is infinite blessedness and happiness. Nothing can be added to make him more blessed and happy. God is always the same. That is his name. 'But you are the same' (*Ps.* 102:27). All existing things add nothing to God, nor do they change him. His blessedness, happiness and self-satisfaction as well as all his other infinite perfections were absolutely the same before as well as after the creation of all things. Nothing that he called into existence added one tiny bit to his infinite blessedness and happiness.

In God's Being there are three persons, Father, Son and Holy Spirit and in their love and fellowship together lie all the happiness and blessedness of God. So before there was any revelation of God in creation, God was, in his infinite Being and goodness, eternally blessed in the knowledge and enjoyment of his own Being and its existence in the three distinct persons of the Godhead.

This God, in his infinite Being and goodness, by his own will and pleasure, guided by infinite wisdom and ena-bled by almighty power, created all things. And to all creatures he communicated a finite, limited, dependent being. God created all things and gave them being and existence out of nothing. He spoke the word and they came into existence. And he saw that they were 'exceed-ingly good' (*Gen.* 1:31). In creation, then, infinite goodness, wisdom and power are gloriously revealed.

In this state, all created things depended on God him-self, on the grace of his perseverance and on his power. And their continued dependence on God was by virtue of the principle which God implanted in their natures so that they would fulfil the purpose for which they were made.

Thus, 'in the beginning God created the heavens and the earth'. He created for himself two distinct, rational families, dependent on him, under a moral law, obedience to which would bring glory to him. The earth he created for man, which suited human nature in every way, in the preservation of his existence and in enabling him to fulfil the purpose of his creation which was to give glory to God. Heaven he created for angels, which was suited for them, for the preservation of their existence, and the purpose for which they were created which was also to glorify God.

To man, God gave power and dominion over all things here below to use them all to glorify God. By man's using creation rightly and thanking God for all that He had created for his use, God received glory from the animal and even the inanimate creation. The angels had similar dominion over the heavenly and spiritual bodies which God had created for their happiness and good, that through the study of them and the use of them, God might receive glory and praise not only from the angels but also from the objects of their praise.

Scripture does not support the idea that there are other intelligent creatures besides angels and men. That idea disturbs the whole representation of the glory of God and the whole purpose of his wisdom and grace declared in Scripture. The existence of other intellectual creatures besides angels and men is the creation of the fanciful imaginations of sinful men who have lost all semblance of wisdom.

This order of things was 'exceedingly good'. Both angels and men lived in dependence on God. He was the head of both families. Nothing was communicated to them except what they received directly from God himself. And this union and fellowship among themselves lay in this alone, that they all obeyed God.

This union between the two families of God was disturbed and dissolved by sin. Part of the heavenly family and the entire earthly family ceased to be dependent on God, and because they were no longer centred on him as their head, they fell out with each other and lived in enmity among themselves. So, to show that its goodness was lost, God cursed the earth and all that was in it, for it was all put in subjection to man, when he had not yet fallen away from God. Nevertheless, God did not curse the heavens which were subject to the angels, because only some of them rebelled against God. The rest of the angels who did not rebel continued to live in their heavenly state. But mankind in its entirety had fallen away from God.

The angels that sinned God utterly rejected for ever, as an example of his severity. But the whole human race God would not utterly cast off. He determined to save a number of them, according to the election of grace.

But God did not intend to restore them to their former state, to two distinct families, each directly dependent upon him. Instead, he planned to gather them both into one, under a new head, by whom the angels would be kept from sinning and the elect chosen from the human race, delivered from the curse which sin had brought upon them. In the meantime he leaves them to live in their different and distinct dwelling places (*Eph.* 3:15).

This is what Paul teaches in Ephesians. He tells us 'that in the dispensation of the fullness of the times' he will 'gather together in one all things in Christ, both which are in heaven and which are on earth—in Him' (*Eph.* 1:10). Colossians 1:20 tells us that God would 'reconcile all things to Himself, by Him [Christ], whether things on earth or things in heaven, having made peace through the blood of His cross'.

This new head, in whom God purposed to gather up all things in heaven and earth into one family, and on whom all things were to depend and by whom they would be held together, is Jesus Christ, the Son of God incarnate (*1 Cor.* 11:3, *Eph.* 1:22-23). This glory was reserved for him. There was no other good enough or fit enough for this glorious work (*Col.* 1:17-19).

To enable Christ to carry out this work, all power in heaven and earth, all fullness of grace and glory were given to him. God now communicates with his new family only through their new head, Jesus Christ. In him this new family is held together; on him all its members depend; to him they owe their submission. In their relation to him lie all peace, union and agreement among themselves. This is what Paul means by God 'reconciling' or 'gathering all things together' by Christ.

But each part of the new family is dealt with separately by Christ. Mankind needed redemption and grace. The angels did not. The good angels were confirmed in glory. We are not, and will not be until we get to heaven.

Christ took our nature into union with his own in order that he might repair it so that once again it can live to glorify God. But he did not take upon himself the nature of angels (*Heb.* 2:14-16). He unites us to himself by his Spirit which exalts us to a dignity and honour making us fit to have fellowship with the angels in one family.

So, as the head of this new family including both angels and the redeemed together, Christ is exceedingly glorious—far above our understanding. Nevertheless the following will help us to see something of his glory in this work.

Christ's glory is seen in the fact that he alone was fit and able to be the head of this new family. He alone could bear the weight of this glory. No creature was fit to be made the head of God's new creation, and to have all things dependent on him so that there should be no communication between God and the creature except by and through him alone. So when the Holy Spirit assigns this glory to Christ he describes him as 'the brightness of the Father's glory, and the express image of his person, and upholding all things by the word of his power' (*Heb.* 1:3). 'He is the image of the invisible God, the first-born over all creation. For by him all things were created that are in heaven and that are on earth, visible and invisible, whether thrones or dominions or principalities or powers. All things were created through him and for him. And he is before all things, and in him all things consist' (*Col.* 1:15-17). Only Christ, and no other, was fit to bear and uphold this glory. The glory of his person is such that the blessedness of all creatures depends on their being centred on him in his glorious office as head of the new family in heaven and earth.

This, then, is the glory which God purposed to give to his only incarnate Son. Here we have an insight into God's purpose to glorify himself in the incarnation of Christ. God purposed that his eternal, only begotten Son would be made man.

What did God purpose to accomplish by this incomprehensible work of his wisdom, love and power?

By the incarnation of Christ, God intended first of all to

redeem the church by the sacrifice of his Son. But there is a greater reason for the incarnation of Christ, one which centres on the glory of God. This was that he might 'gather all things into one' in Christ. The whole creation, especially that which was to be eternally blessed, was to have a new head given to it. From him all graces were to flow into this new family, and from this new family worship, praise and gratitude would flow back to him. All communications from God to this new family would be channelled through Christ, and all worship and gratitude to God from this new family would also be channelled through Christ. Who can describe the divine beauty, order and harmony of all things in this new family under its new head Jesus Christ? The union and communion between angels and men, the order of the whole family in heaven and earth, the communication of life, grace, power, mercy and comfort to the church and all things being ruled for the glory of God all depend on Jesus Christ. This glory God purposed for his incarnate Son, and it was the greatest, the highest glory that could be given to him.

If we thought more of this glory of Christ, and of the wisdom of God in the restoration of all things in Christ, how much more diligent we would be in fulfilling our duties, and how full of gratitude we would be for the glorious privilege of being in this new family!

In particular, the Lord Christ is glorified in his repairing the violation of the glory of God in creation by sin. How beautifully ordered all things were as they lived and moved in dependence on God. But sin destroyed this order and harmony. But all is restored, repaired and made up in this restoration of all things in our new head, Jesus

Christ. Now divine creation is made more beautiful than it was before. So all creation groans as it longs for this glorious restoration of all things.

In this work of restoration, Christ is also glorious because he is appointed as the only way by which all the treasures of the infinite wisdom of God towards his creatures are opened up and revealed. In the first creation, infinite wisdom was the inseparable companion of infinite power. 'How marvellous are your works, O Lord! In wisdom you have made them all.' But when the effects of this divine wisdom were defaced by sin, greater treasures of wisdom were required to repair the damage done. And in this restoration of all things in Christ, God showed what he intended to do in dealing with his creatures. By his restoration of all things under one head, the manifold, unsearchable wisdom of God was made known to the angels themselves (*Eph.* 3:10). They had no idea previously of what God intended to do after sin had entered into the world. They had no idea how God would repair the damage done by sin. But by this purpose to gather together all things in Christ, the manifold wisdom of God was made known to them. So, in Christ 'are hid', and by him are gloriously displayed, 'all the treasures of wisdom' (*Col.* 2:3). In this he is glorious and will be for ever.

The glory of Christ is also seen in the stability and security that is given to the whole new creation. The first creation was glorious. But everything depended on God under a covenant of obedience. Everything was brought down by the sin of angels and men. But now everything that belongs to this new creation, including every believer in the world, as well as the angels in heaven, being gathered together under this one head, are all infallibly kept from ever being ruined by sin again. In this new head all is 'established, strengthened and settled', and that for ever (*1 Pet.* 5:10).

12: *The First Difference between Beholding the Glory of Christ by Faith and by Sight*

Faith and sight are the two spiritual powers of our souls (*2 Cor.* 5:7). The view which we have of the glory of Christ by faith in this world is like looking into a mirror (*1 Cor.* 13:12). In a mirror we do not see the actual person but only an image of him which is imperfect.

The shadow or image of this glory of Christ is drawn for us in the gospel. There we behold him as if we were seeing him only in a mirror. We see only his image or representation. By using this picture of looking into a mirror, Paul declares the comparative imperfection of our present view of the glory of Christ. But this glass which Paul talks about, could also refer to something like a telescope by which we are able to see things more clearly which are at a great distance from us. The gospel functions in this way. Without it we could never know anything of Christ at all. But in using it we are still far from beholding the true dimensions of his glory.

This 'seeing through a glass darkly' could also refer to words, especially to riddles or 'dark sayings' (*Ps.* 78:2). But the gospel itself is not dark or obscure. It is clear, plain and direct. In the gospel Christ is clearly set forth as crucified, exalted and glorified. But Paul is not talking about how the revelation of Christ's glory *comes to us* but the means or instrument by which *we come to understand* that revelation. This is our faith, which is weak and imperfect and understands the glory of Christ very imperfectly and with difficulty.

While on earth 'we walk by faith and not by sight' (*2 Cor.* 5:7, see also *Song of Sol.* 2:9). There is, as it were, a wall between us and Christ. Christ looks at us through the windows of the ordinances of the gospel. Through the promises of the gospel we get further views of him. So our sight of the glory of Christ which we have in this world by faith is weak, transient, imperfect and partial. We are like Job who said, 'Look, I go forward, but he is not there, and backward, but I cannot perceive him; when he works on the left hand, I cannot behold him; when he turns to the right hand I cannot see him' (*Job* 23:8-9).

Now let us compare the sight of Christ's glory which we have by faith, with the vision or sight of that glory of Christ which we shall have in heaven.

In heaven we shall no longer have merely an image, a representation of Christ such as we have in the gospel. We 'shall see him', says Paul, 'face to face' (*1 Cor.* 13:12). 'We shall see him as he is,' says John (*1 John* 3:2). As a man sees his neighbour face to face, so we shall see the Lord Christ in glory, and not like Moses who saw only the 'back parts' of God. In heaven our physical eyes will be cured (see *Job* 19:25-27).

But this vision we shall have of Christ in heaven will be chiefly intellectual. It is not, therefore, the human nature of Christ that is the object of heavenly vision, but his divine person. I have no idea what understanding and sight we shall have of the union of Christ's two natures. But this I do know: in the actual sight of Christ, we shall see a glory in this union of his two natures a thousand times more wonderful than we can conceive. The glories of infinite wisdom, love and power will be continually before us and all the glories of the person of Christ himself will be seen by us for ever. So our eternal blessedness is, that 'we shall always be with the Lord' (*1 Thess.* 4:17).

There will also be a subjective glory in us as we see the glory of Christ. John says, 'It has not yet been revealed what we shall be' (*1 John* 3:2). Who can understand what glory will be ours when we behold this glory of Christ? And how excellent then must that glory of Christ itself be! The actual sight of Christ is what all the saints of God desire in this life more than anything else—to depart to be with Christ (*Phil.* 1:23); 'to be absent from the body and present with the Lord' (*2 Cor.* 5:8). Those who do not long for this sight of Christ's glory as their highest joy are unspiritual and blind.

In order to see the glory of Christ our present physical eyes will be given a new power. Without this power we cannot see him as he is. When he was transfigured on the Mount, the disciples were bewildered rather than comforted (*Matt.* 17:6). They saw his glory, but said foolish things in response (*Luke* 9:30-33). This was because their present sight could not behold the real glory of Christ. Similarly, when John saw the glorified Christ 'he fell at his feet as dead' (*Rev.* 1:17). Paul also 'fell to the ground' (*Acts* 26:13-14).

The church in this life is no way fit to have fellowship with Christ by direct sight, in spite of the grace imparted to it. And therefore those who dream of his personal reign on earth before the day of judgement are talking nonsense unless they believe that all the saints will then be glorified also. This is why it is abominable to try to represent the glory of Christ by pictures and images.

The only thing for which we are presently suited is to have Christ dwell with us and in us by his Spirit. Under the Old Testament Christ's glory was represented by fleshly ordinances. And while on earth his true glory was hidden by his human flesh. But now, says Paul, 'We know Christ no more according to the flesh,' neither as they did under the Old Testament nor as they did in the days of his flesh (*2 Cor.* 5:16). For when Christ left the earth, he sent his Spirit (*John* 16:7), by whom the disciples had a clearer view of the glory of Christ than they could have had by beholding him in the flesh. That is our condition today.

In heaven, the mind shall be freed from the darkness brought on it by sin. It will be a glorious aid to faith rather than a hindrance. Under the power of sin the mind was completely unable to discern spiritual things rightly. This inability is to some extent removed by grace, so that those who were darkness become light in the Lord; they have a new spiritual light communicated to them. But in heaven the mind will have a clear, unclouded understanding and sight of the glory of Christ.

On earth our minds are also hindered by the flesh which is corrupt and subject to sickness, tiredness and old age. But in heaven a new light, the light of glory, shall be implanted in the mind. Man has in him now a natural light enabling him to discern the things of man, an ability to know, perceive and judge natural things. This is that 'spirit of a man, which is the lamp of the Lord, searching all the inner depths of the heart' (*Prov.* 20:27). But this light does not enable us to discern spiritual things aright (*1 Cor.* 2:11-15). So God gives a greater light, a supernatural light of faith and grace, to those whom he effectually calls to the knowledge of his glory in the face of his dear Son. This new light does not make the light of nature useless or redundant. Rather this new light directs it and guides it to fulfil its true purpose. Yet this light is of quite another nature.

But even this new light enables us to see the glory of Christ in this world only very imperfectly. But in heaven there shall be a supernatural light of glory added. And as the light of grace does not destroy or make redundant the light of nature but rather rectifies and improves it, so the light of glory does not destroy or make redundant this light of faith and grace, but makes it absolutely perfect. As by the light of nature we cannot truly understand the light of grace, so by the light of grace we cannot fully understand the light of glory. The best idea we can have of this light of glory is that it perfectly transforms the soul into the image and likeness of Christ. This is how we are brought to rest and blessedness. Grace renews nature and glory perfects grace. So the whole soul is brought to its rest in God.

We have a picture of this in Christ's healing of the blind man (*Matt.* 8:22-24). This man was completely blind. Then his eyes were opened, but he could not see clearly. He saw men like trees walking. But then, at the second touch, he saw clearly. So, our minds are blind. Grace gives them a partial sight of spiritual things. But the light of glory gives perfect sight and understanding.

The glorified body will also play its part. In our resurrected, glorified bodies we shall see our Redeemer with glorified eyes. We do not know what power and spirituality our glorified bodies will possess. But it is clear they will play a part in our eternal blessedness. While still on earth, Stephen 'saw the glory of God, and Jesus standing at the right hand of God' (*Acts* 7:55-56). If this is what he was enabled to see while still in this body, what power of sight shall we have in eternal glory?

Christ himself indicated how great a privilege it was to see him on earth (*Matt.* 13:17). How much greater a privilege it is then to see Christ in eternal glory!

These are some of the differences between our beholding Christ by faith here and by direct sight in heaven.

Here we often struggle. We 'who have the first-fruits of the Spirit, even we groan within ourselves, eagerly waiting for the adoption, the redemption of our body' (*Rom.* 8:23). The more we grow in faith and spiritual light, the more we groan for deliverance. The nearer we are to heaven and to Christ, the more earnest is our desire to be there, and to be with Christ. Groaning implies a strong desire, mixed with sorrow, because we do not yet have what we long for. The desire has sorrow in it, but the sorrow has joy in it, like a heavy shower of rain falling on us on a Spring day while we are in a garden. We get wet, but when we smell and see what the shower has done, we are happy even though we groan because we are soaked through! So groaning shows we long to be delivered from our present state and be lifted up to that heavenly glorious state (see *Rom.* 7:24).

In longing for this perfect sight of Christ we can learn from the saints in the Old Testament. The sight which they had of the glory of Christ (for they also saw his glory obscurely through their ordinances and sacrifices) was weak and imperfect even in the most enlightened believers. It was much inferior to what we now have by faith through the gospel. Yet they were encouraged to study and search diligently into what was revealed (*1 Pet.* 1:10-11). Nevertheless, what they learned was dark and confused. And the continuance of this veil on the revelation of the glory of Christ, while a veil of ignorance and blindness was upon their hearts and minds, proved the ruin of that church in its apostasy (*2 Cor.* 3:7, 13-14). This double veil God promised to take away (*Isa.* 25:7). And then they shall turn to the Lord; then they shall be able to behold clearly the glory of Christ (*2 Cor.* 3:16).

But real believers among them desired and prayed for these veils to be removed so that 'the Sun of Righteousness should arise with healing in his wings'. Their spiritual wisdom was outstanding. They rejoiced and gloried in the ordinances of divine worship which they did enjoy. Yet they longed for this removal, so that they might enjoy the reality they symbolized. But those who did not desire this, but trusted in their present institutions, were not accepted with God. Meanwhile those spiritually illuminated looked for the revelation of the whole mystery of the wisdom of God in Christ, as did the angels (*1 Pet.* 1:3, *Eph.* 3:9-10).

So there was more of the power of true faith and love under the Old Testament than is found among most Christians today. They saw the promises afar off, were persuaded by them, and embraced them (*Heb.* 11:13). Simeon is a great example (*Luke* 2:28-29).

Our present darkness and weakness in beholding the glory of Christ is not like theirs. His glory is not hid from us as it was under the Old Testament. Nor does our poor vision arise from the lack of a clear revelation of the person and office of Christ.

But it is hid from us by the nature of faith itself in comparison with actual sight and it is hid by the way it is brought to us, 'through a glass darkly', that is, we see by faith only an image and not the reality. But in heaven all will be clear and the sight of Christ will indeed be glorious. Now if Old Testament saints prayed and desired the removal of the divine ordinances of worship so that they could see the reality of what they symbolized, how much more should we pray and desire the removal of all weakness, all darkness and of everything that prevents us now from seeing Christ in reality.

So to sum up. There are three things concerning the seeing of the glory of Christ. There is the shadow, the perfect image and the reality itself. Those under the law had the shadow. They did not have the perfect image (*Heb.* 10:1). Under the gospel we have the perfect image, which they did not have. We have a clear, complete revelation and declaration of it in Scripture. But the actual enjoyment of the reality is reserved for us in heaven.

If, then, those under the Old Testament longed to be freed from their state of types and shadows to enjoy the glory of Christ represented to us in the gospel, how much more ought we to desire and pray to be delivered from our present state so that we may enjoy the reality in heaven.

Let us then examine ourselves. Do we long and desire to see the reality of Christ's glory in heaven? Are we meditating on that perfect image of Christ's glory given to us in the gospel? Or are we too filled with this world and its concerns? As believers, beholding the glory of Christ in the glass of the gospel, we are changed into the same image and likeness by the Spirit of the Lord. So those beholding the beauty of the world and the things that are in it through the cursed glass of self-love are in their minds changed into its image. But we have not so learned Christ Jesus.

13: *The Second Difference between Beholding the Glory of Christ by Faith and by Sight*

While we are in this life, the Lord Christ is pleased, in his sovereign wisdom, sometimes to withdraw, and, as it were, to hide himself from us. When this happens it is as if clouds and darkness cover our minds. Faith is helpless. We cannot behold his glory. We seek him, but we cannot find him. This was Job's complaint (*Job* 23:8-9). The church also complains that God is a God who hides himself (*Isa.* 45:15). The psalmist similarly asks how long God will continue to hide himself (*Ps.* 89:46).

This hiding of the face of God is the hiding of his glory which shines in the face of Jesus Christ, and therefore of the glory of Christ himself, since his glory is to show forth the glory of God. Men may still hold a right doctrine of Christ; but beholding the glory of Christ does not lie in remembering doctrine. Men may have the outward form of godliness but no longer have the encouragement of Christ's presence and glory.

From this two questions arise. (i) Why does the Lord Christ sometimes hide himself and his glory from the faith of believers? (ii) How may we know that he has withdrawn himself?

(i) In answering the first question we must know that Christ is governed by his sovereign wisdom. Yet there are many holy reasons why he does withdraw himself. I shall only mention one. He withdraws himself in order to make us appreciate him more so that we diligently seek for him as we would seek for a lost precious treasure.

We all too easily take Christ for granted and become lazy in seeking fellowship with him. Christ is very patient with us even though we treat him so unkindly. It is only because he is so gracious that he merely withdraws himself rather than leaves us for ever. He knows that those who have beheld his glory in some measure, although they have not valued it as they should, cannot bear it when his presence and the sight of his glory are withdrawn. So, by withdrawing himself he aims to awaken his people to search for him, and to mourn over their sin in taking him for granted.

We are like the man in the parable the prophet told Ahab. A prisoner of war had been committed to the care of the prophet, but while he was busy here and there, his prisoner escaped (*1 Kings* 20:35-43). Christ commits himself to us, and we ought carefully to keep him with us and treasure the sight of his glory which we have by faith. 'I held him', says the Shulamite, symbolizing the church, 'and would not let him go' (*Song of Sol.* 3:4). But while we are busy with other things, Christ withdraws himself and we cannot find him. Yet even this discipline is for our recovery and sanctification.

(ii) Our second question is how we may know when Christ withdraws himself. Here we are concerned only with those who are troubled about the liveliness of their faith and love to Christ above all things. They are concerned about their whole walk with God. The simple answer is that we may know Christ has withdrawn himself by the sad consequences that follow.

The first consequence concerns the life and strength of

grace in us. So long as we behold the glory of Christ grace is lively and strong. While we enjoy the presence of Christ we live. Christ lives in us by his Spirit, stirring up grace and strengthening it in us (*2 Cor.* 3:18). Of course it is impossible for grace to languish while Christ is present and his glory is seen. But without his presence with us and without a sight of his glory, all doctrinal knowledge of him is dry and useless. Any view we have of his glory is but fanciful imagination or superstition without any transforming power. But if we behold his glory we grow more and more in grace, holiness and obedience.

Many people have tried to recover a sight of Christ's glory by making images, crucifixes and pictures of him. By these their outward senses may be stirred but their hearts remain untouched; they become as wooden as their images. They substitute the outward forms and observances which they diligently perform but all the while they deny the inward power of godliness.

However, we learn from these attempts to behold the glory of Christ by images that all professing Christians feel they must somehow or other behold the glory of Christ in order to love him and be made like him. But just here lies the difference. The church of Rome says it can be done by beholding crucifixes, images and pictures of him with our physical eyes, whereas we say that we can behold the glory of Christ only by faith as he is revealed in the gospel and in no other way. Images only serve to turn the minds of men away from Christ. They can never satisfy a truly spiritual man. Images are pleasing only to the spiritually dead and to the superstitious.

So the first consequence of Christ's withdrawing himself

from us is that inward graces grow weak and we tend to rely more and more on outside helps. Above all, we lose the desire for holy meditation and we spend less and less time with Christ. Just as frost withers the plants in the garden, so the grace in our hearts also withers when the 'Sun of Righteousness' withdraws and hides himself.

When we find a spiritual deadness and coldness in our souls and no joy in religious duties, then we know that Christ has withdrawn himself. Some claim that we need to be constantly revived by the Holy Spirit. Unless he constantly falls as dew and showers on our dry and barren hearts, unless he causes our graces to thrive, unless he revives and increases faith, love and holiness in our souls, our backslidings will not be healed nor will our spiritual state be recovered. This is why he is prayed for and promised in Scripture (see *Song of Sol.* 4:16, *Isa.* 44:3-4, *Ezek.* 11:19, 36, *Hos.* 14:5-6). This is true. But how does the Holy Spirit revive our souls and strengthen our graces? By stirring us up to behold the glory *of Christ*. 'We', says Paul, 'beholding the glory of Christ as in a glass, are changed into the same image from glory to glory, even by the Spirit of the Lord.' It is as the Holy Spirit gets us to behold the glory *of Christ* by faith that he powerfully renews and transforms our souls.

Some complain of their sad spiritual state. Some make great self-efforts to revive their souls, such as imposing on themselves many religious duties. But if they would only behold the glory of Christ by faith as he is revealed to us in the Scriptures they would soon be healed. If only they would abide in Christ, then they would be fruitful (*John* 15:4-5).

There are two reasons for coming to Christ by faith. The first is to receive life and salvation. But secondly, we come to him as believers so that we may have 'life more abundantly' (*John* 10:10). That is, to receive such supplies of grace as may keep our souls spiritually healthy and strong. And as Christ reproves those who would not come to him that they might have life, so also he reproves those who do not come to him by faith for abundant life.

When the Lord Christ is near us and we do, by faith, behold his glory then he fills our hearts with joy and peace in believing. He is like a refreshing drink to a thirsty soul. When the 'Sun of Righteousness' arises in the soul, then we find there is 'healing under his wings'. His beams of grace by the Holy Spirit bring strength and renewed vigour to the soul, for by these graces Christ comes to us as Comforter through his Spirit.

Many love to have only the outward form of godliness and could not care less about evangelical privileges. They do not seek the marrow of divine promises which is the very life of communion with Christ. They are not concerned whether they have spiritual peace, refreshing comforts, unspeakable joys or the blessed peace of assurance. Without some taste and experience of these things, the Christian life is heartless, lifeless and useless and religion itself becomes a lifeless corpse. The peace which some enjoy is mere stupidity. It is a great evidence of the power of unbelief that we can be happy without experiencing the reality of Christ's presence in us by his Spirit. We can be quite happy without any of the joy, peace, comfort or assurance which are promised in the gospel.

How can we possibly believe the promises concerning

heaven, immortality and glory, when we do not believe the promises concerning our present life? And how can we be trusted when we say we believe these promises but make no effort to experience them ourselves? It is just here that men deceive themselves. It is not that they do not want the gospel privileges of joy, peace and assurance, but they are not prepared to repent of their evil attitudes and careless life-styles. Some have even attempted to reconcile these things, and ruined their souls. But without the diligent exercise of the grace of obedience, we shall never enjoy the graces of joy, peace and assurance.

It is specially as we behold the glory of Christ that we experience joy, peace and assurance. These are part of the royal train of his graces. So where Christ is, these graces are not lacking. Study the following verses: Song of Solomon 7:12; John 14:21-23; Revelation 3:20. In the last verse we learn that when he enters into a person's soul he sits down to a fellowship meal, which can only mean that he brings spiritual food and refreshment with him.

So how do we receive these graces of Christ? We receive them by our beholding the glory of Christ by faith (*1 Pet.* 1:8-9).

But many deny that there is any such spiritual fellowship with Christ. They deny the outpouring of the love of God in our hearts by the Holy Spirit, and also the witnessing of the Spirit of God with our spirits that we are the children of God. They make all religion a mere outward show, a pageant more fit for a stage than for that temple of God which is in the minds of men.

Others dare not deny the truth of these spiritual realities but yet make no effort to experience them. As long as they carry out the outward duties of religion they are satisfied. They find their joy and peace in outward performance. But what a sorry joy and peace it is! Such people are spiritually lazy and are really unbelievers. The outward form without the inward reality is inconsistent. If you are satisfied with the one, you will not seek your happiness, joy and peace in the other (*Phil.* 3:8-9).

So, let us not bring dishonour to the gospel by thinking that faith in it and obedience to it bring only trouble, persecution and unpopularity and not joy, peace or assurance. Such thoughts are contrary to the promises of Christ and to the whole teaching of the New Testament (see *Mark* 10:30, *Heb.* 10:34). If we only experience the trouble but not the comforts of the gospel, we must lay the blame squarely on our own shoulders.

How, then, can we behold the glory of Christ? We need, firstly, a spiritual understanding of his glory as revealed in Scripture. Secondly, we need to think much about him if we wish to enjoy him fully (*1 Pet.* 1:8). If we are satisfied with vague ideas about him we shall find no transforming power communicated to us. But when we cling wholeheartedly to him and our minds are filled with thoughts of him and we constantly delight ourselves in him, then spiritual power will flow from him to purify our hearts, increase our holiness, strengthen our graces, and sometimes fill us 'with joy inexpressible and full of glory'.

Where the light of revelation is not accompanied by spiritual experience and power in our souls, then it will end either in outward formality or atheism. But when feelings outrun the light of revelation, then they sink into the bog of superstition, doting on images and pictures. But where there is spiritual restraint and discipline, it is better that our emotions exceed our light, rather than light exceed our emotions. It is by the defect of our understanding that we do not have more light and it is by the corruption of our wills that we do not have more experience of spiritual comforts.

Ungoverned passions and emotions greatly hinder the mind from working properly, even in natural and moral thoughts. How much more, then, will they prevent us from thinking aright about spiritual things and create a barrier to the preaching of the gospel.

Some have a satanic blindness on their minds which makes it impossible for them to behold anything of the glory of Christ (*2 Cor.* 4:3-4). But all of us have a corrupt, natural darkness on our minds, a mental depravity which prevents us from beholding the glory of Christ. So 'the light shines in darkness, and the darkness did not comprehend it' (*John* 1:5).

Paul tells us that 'the natural man does not receive the things of the Spirit of God, for they are foolishness to him; nor can he know them, for they are spiritually discerned' (*1 Cor.* 2:14). This is why so few respond to the preaching of the gospel. There are few who discern any glory or beauty in Christ that they should desire him (*Isa.* 53:1-2). No man is able of himself to receive Christ and behold his glory. The power of grace must remove the darkness and blindness from his mind. Yet some are more opposed to the preaching of the gospel than others and this is because of their lusts and corruptions.

Then there are those whose understanding has been enlightened to perceive and discern spiritual things (*Eph.*

1:16-18). But this enlightenment is only partial in this world (*1 Cor.* 13:12). Some are more enlightened than others. But however much we are enlightened our corrupt nature is ready and waiting to obstruct our view of the glory of Christ by such things as love for the world, sensual pleasures and other things which weaken our spiritual ability to behold the glory of Christ.

So we have, by faith, a view of the glory of Christ. This view is weak and unstable due to the nature of faith itself and the way the glory of Christ is presented to it, that is, by the Scriptures, which is like viewing an object some distance away through dark glasses. The light of faith in the mind is also darkened by our lusts and corruptions which need to be continually mortified. This is why meditation is so difficult and why the preaching of Christ is so unprofitable to so many.

The one who has seen something of the glory of Christ will count everything else as 'rubbish', that he might know Christ better and see more of his glory (*Phil.* 3:8-10). A spiritual sight of Christ will fill the heart with love for him. So, if any one does not love Christ that person has never seen Christ and does not know him at all. When we fall in love with someone we often think about them. So, when we fall in love with Christ we will be constantly thinking about him. And where a person is not filled with thoughts of Christ, that person only deceives himself if he claims to have received him as Saviour.

Our lusts and corruptions have the power to deflect us from Christ, and, in addition, Satan is always ready to darken our minds and hinder our faith by his many temptations. His aim is to blind the eyes of men 'lest the light of the glorious gospel of Christ, who is the image of God, should shine on them' (*2 Cor.* 4:4). However glorious is the light of the gospel by the preaching of the Word, by various means and subtle tricks Satan blinds the minds of most who hear it so that they cannot behold the glory of Christ in it. In this way, he continues to rule the children of disobedience. But God overpowers Satan so that he cannot continue to blind his elect. He shines into their hearts to give them the knowledge of his glory in the face of Jesus Christ. Yet Satan will never give up. He will always try to darken the minds even of believers so that they find it difficult to maintain their clear sight of the glory of Christ. And this he does in two ways.

With some, Satan arouses fears, doubts, arguments, uncertainties and various worries and troubles, so that believers find it difficult to maintain comforting views of Christ or his glory. He tempts them to fear that they have been rejected and cast off by Christ. So their anxieties are increased and they are driven to the edge of despair.

Satan deceives others into a false assurance by which they promise peace to themselves, and so live in a vague presumption that they will be saved by Christ even though they have no idea how. This is why Paul presses on Christians the duty of self-examination (*2 Cor.* 13:15). We must ask ourselves whether Christ is in us or not. And he cannot be in us unless he has been received by that faith with which we behold his glory. For by faith we receive him and by faith he dwells in our hearts (*John* 1:12, *Eph.* 3:17). By deceiving people in this way, Satan prevails in the world.

But what of the sight of the glory of Christ that we shall have in heaven compared to the sight we have here on earth? It will be clear and stable. Nothing will interrupt or be able to draw our eyes away from it, for we shall have been delivered from sin and from everything that now hinders our view of Christ.

Consider the state of our minds in glory. The faculties of our souls shall then be made perfect as all 'the spirits of just men' are (*Heb.* 12:23). David said, 'As for me, I will see your face in righteousness. I shall be satisfied when I awake in your likeness.' Christ alone is the likeness and image of God. When we awake in the other world, with our minds purified and rectified, then we shall always be satisfied because we shall always be beholding him and his glory. Our minds and eyes will never get tired; we shall be like the four living creatures which 'do not rest day or night, saying, "Holy, holy, holy, Lord God Almighty, who was and is and is to come!"' In heaven we shall be continually admiring and praising God in Christ, never needing any rest or even being interrupted. We shall be like the angels.

Nor shall we need any spectacles or visual aids or helps to behold the glory of Christ in heaven! Our bodily eyes will be glorified and strengthened to bear the sight for ever. This is much better than faith. This sight will be aided by a new internal power, or an act of the internal power of our minds with which we shall be endowed in the glorified state. By this power we shall be able to 'see him face to face', to see him as he is. We will be able to behold the glory of Christ directly. This sight of Christ's glory will never vary. We will never need to rest our eyes and minds by sleep!

The next wonder will be that the Lord Christ will never

again—not even for one second—withdraw himself from us. 'We shall always be with the Lord' (*1 Thess.* 4:7). This will be the greatest difference between the good and the evil in their future states. Eternity makes the elect absolutely good and the reprobate absolutely evil. To be in hell under the wrath of God is in itself the greatest punishment, but to be there for ever with no relief from present misery and no hope of ever being freed from eternal misery makes it even more terrible. So is the joy and blessedness of eternal life in heaven beholding the glory of Christ. 'We shall always be with the Lord', not limited by time and with no interruption of our enjoyment of God in Christ.

In heaven there is no need of instituted forms of worship, nor ordinances of divine service (*Rev.* 21:22). Neither has it any need of the sun or moon to shine in it. For the glory of God and of the Lamb will be its light. On this earth the gospel sometimes shines as gloriously as the sun and at other times as the light of the moon. But in heaven the perpetual presence of Christ with his saints makes it always as glorious as the sun shining in all its might.

Neither will this vision be weakened by internal corruptions nor from any temptations. No doubts or fears or disturbing thoughts will have any place in heaven, but only that which will strengthen us and lead us to behold the glory of Christ with satisfied delight.

So the sight of Christ's glory in heaven will always be the same, always new, never growing old and out of date. The mind will never be disturbed by, or diverted from, or bored with the sight. All the faculties of our souls will be fixed on Christ's glory for ever.

So when in this life we have glorious views of Christ by faith, they ought to make us long after, and desire to come to, this more perfect, abiding and infinitely unchanging sight of Christ's glory in heaven!

14: *The Third Difference between Beholding the Glory of Christ by Faith and by Sight*

The view we have here by faith of the glory of Christ is gathered from Scripture in bits and pieces. These bits and pieces have to be brought together in our minds so that we may have a clear idea of the glory of Christ. We do not have great visions of the glory of Christ as Isaiah had under the Old Testament, and as John had on the isle of Patmos (*Isa.* 6:1-4, *Rev.* 1:13-16). We do not need them. They would not help us. 'We have a more sure word of prophecy,' says Peter (*2 Pet.* 1:17-19). One of those who did receive these glorious visions cried out, 'Woe is me, for I am undone!' The other 'fell as dead at his feet'. In this life we are not able to bear such glorious visions of Christ. And as we do not have glorious visions of him, neither do we have any new revelations of his glory by direct inspiration. Scripture is our only blueprint of the glory of Christ. Only *in* Scripture and only *by* faith can we behold the glory of Christ while still in this life.

Nor does Scripture give us an entire picture of the glory of Christ in a single place. Nor can it do so. If all the lights in our heavens were concentrated into one, it would not help us see better. Instead it would blind us. So divine wisdom distributed the light into sun, moon and stars, each giving out its own measure of light to enlighten the world. So if the whole glory of Christ and all that belongs to that glory had been concentrated into one description, it would have been too much for our minds to take in. We would have been confused and bewildered rather than enlightened. So God has distributed the light of Christ's glory through the whole firmament of the Scriptures. Each part gives off its own light for the building up of the church's faith. One part of Scripture describes his person and glory clearly and plainly, whereas other parts present it in allegories conveying a heavenly sense of them to the minds of believers. Yet other parts describe his glory in terms of his love, his humbling himself for our salvation, his exaltation and his power. As one star differs from another in glory, so God revealed the glory of Christ under the Old Testament types and shadows, and more fully under the New Testament. Glorious testimonies to these things are planted in all parts of Scripture which we might gather as Eve might have gathered flowers in the paradise of God.

The Shulamite in the Song of Solomon, having considered every part of her beloved, concludes that 'he is altogether lovely' (5:10-16). So we ought to study Scripture to find out all that is revealed to us of the glory of Christ, as did the prophets of old (*1 Pet.* 1:11).

Those who make gilded images of Christ only 'feed on ashes', and hold 'a lie in their right hand'. In Scripture, Jesus Christ is clearly set before us as crucified (*Gal.* 3:1). So also by Scripture we see him exalted and glorified. And it is the wisdom of faith to gather together all the descriptions of Christ's glory in Scripture so that faith may more clearly behold him.

But in heaven we will always see the whole glory of Christ, and we shall be enabled by one act of the light of glory to understand it as only a glorified creature in heaven can. The vision which we shall have of the glory of Christ in heaven, and of the glory of the immense God in him, will perfectly transform us into the image of Christ. When we see him we shall be like him, for we shall see him as he is (*1 John* 3:2).

When, at death, the soul departs from the body, it is immediately freed from all weakness, disability, darkness, doubts and fears. The image of the first Adam will then be abolished. All physical weaknesses and infirmities will have gone for ever. This necessarily follows death, in order that we may enter into that blessed state. The first entry into immortality from mortality is a step towards eternal glory and into eternal rest. The great evil, death, thus becomes the means of freeing us from all the remains of evil in us. It is by virtue of the death of Christ alone that the souls of believers are freed by death from the presence of sin and all the effects that sin had wrought on their bodies, and being freed their souls flourish and expand to their fullest extent.

But it is not so with the wicked. Death to them is a curse, for it plunges them into eternal misery and pain. They will be for ever deprived of all the comforts they had in this world. Their souls, separated from their bodies, will be continually troubled and harassed by all those evil passions which filled their minds with corrupt fleshly lusts. They look for relief by death in vain.

The 'spirits of just men' are freed by death from their mortal bodies not yet glorified. All the powers of their souls and all the graces in them, such as faith, love and delight, are immediately set free, and enabled constantly to be exercised for the glory and praise of God in Christ.

The purpose of these powers was to enable us to glorify God and enjoy him for ever. When we are freed from the hindrance and encumbrance of the body, they can now fully exert all their powers to the glory of God and the enjoyment of him for ever. And when the body is fully redeemed by its resurrection, it shall be so purified, sanctified and glorified that it will no longer be a hindrance and an encumbrance to the soul. Instead it will be a blessed instrument for the soul's highest and most spiritual activities.

Our eyes were made to see our Redeemer and our other senses to receive all that he communicates to us, according to their capacity. Just as the bodies of the wicked shall be restored to them, to increase and complete their misery in their sufferings, so shall the bodies of the just be restored to them to heighten and complete their blessedness.

These things prepare us for eternal glory. The soul will not be brought into the presence of Christ without a new power enabling it to behold him in the full, blazing light of his glory. Faith ceases for we now no longer behold his glory by faith. The light of glory now replaces faith.

When sin entered the world, God said in grief, upbraiding man for his foolishness, 'Behold, the man is become like one of us!' But when grace has done its glorious work he will say in love and delight as he sees the perfect restoration of his image in man, 'Behold, man has indeed become like one of us.' This is the great result of the light of glory.

This sight of Christ's glory is called the 'Beatific Vision', because it gives perfect rest and blessedness to those who have this sight of Christ.

God in Christ constantly works in glorified souls and communicates his grace to them. All creatures must eternally live, even in heaven, in dependence on him who is the eternal fountain of being, life, goodness and blessedness to all. As we cannot keep ourselves alive for one moment without divine power in us, so in the glorified state we shall depend eternally on divine power and goodness being communicated to us for our eternal blessedness. We have no idea how this is done in heaven even as we have no idea how God communicates his grace to us here on earth. His ways are shrouded in mystery (*John* 3:8).

While we are still on earth, faith, beholding the glory of Christ, will give us a foretaste of future glory. There is no glory, no peace, no joy, no satisfaction to be found in this world compared to what we get from that weak and imperfect view which we have of the glory of Christ by faith. Thus while we are still in this world, faith gives us such a foretaste of future blessedness in the enjoyment of Christ as may continually stir us up to say with the psalmist, 'I shall be satisfied when I awake in your likeness.'

15: *Exhortation to Unbelievers*

Whenever the glory of Christ in his person, grace or office is preached, it should be accompanied with an invitation to sinners to come to him. Christ did this himself (*Matt.* 11:27-30, *John* 7:37-38). So let unbelievers consider the following:

(i) Consider your present relationship to God and to eternity. This is what Moses wished the Israelites would do (*Deut.* 32:39). It is the height of folly to leave these things to chance. Remember, 'many are called but few are chosen'. To be called is to enjoy all the outward privileges of the gospel. To be chosen is to belong to those who will actually be saved. In the parable of the sower, Christ shows that only one of four sorts of hearers was actually saved. So, many deceive themselves, thinking they are saved, but will suddenly be awakened to a sad surprise. And this is pictured by the account of the final judgement, for those who professed to have believed the gospel are revealed as complaining of their disappointments (*Matt.* 25:44-46).

(ii) Beware of being deceived. Without any real evidence, many assume they are Christians, that they are on the right way to heaven, that they are partakers of the outward privileges of the gospel such as hearing the Word, and participating in the sacraments. They have light and convictions, so that they abstain from sin, and they perform duties that others neglect. They compare themselves with others and judge themselves to be much better. This is not the place to preach a sermon on the foolishness of assumptions. But it is important to give this warning: do not trust in these assumptions, for they will eternally deceive your soul. This was the warning John the Baptist gave to the Jews. 'Do not think to say to yourselves, "We have Abraham as our father."' They falsely assumed that because they were the physical descendants of Abraham, they were safe. This false assumption led finally to their ruin. Knowing this, John the Baptist tried to bring them to their senses.

(iii) Consider what it means to live and die without Christ. Without Christ we are at enmity with God and in a state of apostasy, under God's curse and eternal wrath. If we assume all is well with our souls we will not flee to Christ for refuge from eternal damnation. The healthy do not need a doctor. Only the sick come for healing.

Yet however much we preach the danger of dying without Christ, people remain unconcerned.

Preachers must preach these things, yet we know that only a few say, Is this true of me? Tell them that without Christ all their religious duties and activities are useless, and worse, they are rejected by God, and are under his curse and displeasure, and that their final end is eternal destruction, and like Lot's sons-in-law they treat it as a joke (*Gen.* 19:14).

So until you are convinced of your dreadful state without Christ, all that follows will be of no use to you. Remember then that your greatest concern should be the eternal destiny of your soul. If you have a true faith in Christ with evidences of the reality of that faith, that is a matter of eternal praise and thanksgiving. But if not, then you need to be convinced of the dreadful eternity that awaits you without Christ.

The first work necessary for true religion is to be convinced of our dreadful state without Christ. And the great abuse of religion in the world is to pretend one has a true faith when one has not. To think that because one is a practising member of a church, that is sufficient to keep us eternally safe, is a sad delusion. That is a sign we have never been convinced of our lost condition by nature.

(iv) Consider the love of Christ inviting us to come to him for life, deliverance, mercy, grace, peace and eternal salvation. When these invitations are preached today, Jesus Christ still stands before sinners, encouraging them to come to him. Hear him saying to you now, 'Why will you die? Why will you perish and not have pity on your souls? Can you endure that day of wrath that is approaching? Only in a little while and all your hopes, comforts and assumptions will be gone for ever, leaving you eternally miserable. Look to me and be saved. Come to me and I will give rest to your souls. I plead with you to come. Do not shut me out any more. Eternity lies at your door. Cast out all cursed, self-deceiving excuses. Do not so hate me that you would rather perish than be saved by me' (see *Prov.* 1:20-23).

Why does Christ love you? Does he need you? Have you deserved his love? Did you love him first? Can he not be happy and blessed without you? Has he some ulterior motive which makes him so earnest in calling you to him? No, it is nothing but his overflowing mercy, compassion and grace that moves him to call you to himself. So, to treat with contempt Christ's wonderful love and grace to you will lead to your eternal ruin. Who will pity you then?

Objection

But I fear he will not receive me! When I see what a wretched sinner I am, I am afraid that he will turn me away in disgust.

Answer

Christ is ready to receive the worst of sinners who come to him for salvation. All three persons of the Godhead bear testimony to this. Not to receive this testimony makes God a liar. Whatever the Lord Christ is in his person, as the representation of his Father, in his office as mediator, in what he did on earth, in what he now does in heaven—all proclaims the same truth. Nothing but cursed obstinacy in sin and unbelief can suggest to us that he is not willing to receive us when we come to him.

One day preachers will testify against the unbelief of all to whom the gospel was preached, but who did not come to Christ. This unbelief shows great contempt of the wisdom of God, denies his truth or faithfulness, discredits the sincerity of Christ's invitations, and makes him out to be a deceiver. Such unbelief will result in hatred of his person and office, and of the wisdom of God revealed in him. It will end in your eternal destruction in hell. So be warned! You have no excuse for your unbelief.

(v) Consider that he is able to save us as well as being willing to receive us. Generally, this is taken for granted. Christ is able to save us *if he will*. Indeed, who shall question his ability to save us even though we live in sin and unbelief? And many expect him to do so, because they believe he can, *if he will*. But Christ has no such power, nor such ability. He cannot save unbelieving, impenitent sinners, for this cannot be done without denying himself, acting contrary to his Word, and destroying his own glory. So let none deceive himself with such foolish thoughts. Christ is able to save all them, and only them, *who come to God by him*. While you live in sin and unbelief, Christ cannot save you. Christ's power to save those that respond to his call is sovereign and almighty. Nothing and no one can resist it. All things in heaven and earth are committed to him. All power is his, and he will use it to save infallibly all who come to God by him.

(vi) Consider what has been said of Christ as the true representation of God and of all the holy properties of God's nature revealed in Christ. Nothing can possibly give us more encouragement to come to him, for we have shown that God, who is infinitely wise and glorious, has revealed all the holy properties of his nature—his mercy, love, grace, goodness, righteousness, wisdom and power— in Christ and also his purpose to save all who believe in him. Whoever, therefore, comes to Christ by faith because the glory of God is revealed in him truly gives to God the glory which he seeks from his creatures.

There is more glory given to God in coming to Christ by faith, than in keeping the whole law, because Christ has more gloriously revealed the holy properties of God's nature by the salvation of sinners than by the giving of the law. Therefore he who deliberately refuses to come to Christ when called by his Word, secretly shows himself to be a hater of God and one who dislikes his ways and does not wish to see his glory exalted. He chooses rather to die in enmity against him rather than to glorify him. Do not think that it does not really matter whether you come to

Christ or not, or that you can put off coming to Christ till later. Your present refusal of Christ is as high an act of enmity against God as any of which your nature is capable.

(vii) Consider that by coming to Christ you will have a right to all that glory we have been talking about, for Christ will become yours even more intimately than your wife and children belong to you. All his glory will be yours. Christ is nearer to believers than any natural relations are.

Is it a small thing in your eyes, that Christ and all his glory shall be yours, and that this will be your eternal blessedness? Is it nothing to you to continue to despise and neglect this glory? Is it nothing to you to be left to find what happiness you can in this world with its perishing trifles and enter into eternal misery when you die, when such riches of glory are held out to you?

(viii) Finally, consider the horrible ingratitude there is in neglecting or refusing to come to Christ, realizing the eternal ruin that will follow. 'How shall we escape if we neglect so great salvation?' Impenitent unbelievers under the preaching of the gospel are the vilest and most ungrateful of all God's creatures. The devils themselves, as wicked as they are, are not guilty of this sin, for Christ was never offered to them. They were never offered salvation on the condition of faith and repentance. This is the terrible sin of unbelievers and will greatly add to their misery in hell. 'Hear, you despisers, wonder and perish.' The sin of the devil lay in his malice and opposition to knowledge above that which man was given in this world. Man, therefore, must sin in some way above that sin of the devil or God would not give him his eternal portion with the devil and his angels. This sin is unbelief.

Some, it may be, will say, 'What then shall we do? What is required of us?'

(i)   Take the advice of the writer of the Epistle to the Hebrews: 'Today if you will hear his voice, do not harden your hearts as in the rebellion, in the day of trial in the wilderness. But exhort one another daily, while it is called "today", lest any of you be hardened through the deceitfulness of sin.' 'Now is the day of salvation.' Now, at this moment, grace is offered to you. Others have had this day as well as you and have missed their opportunity. Take heed, therefore, lest you too miss your opportunity.

Commit the following to memory: 'Today Christ and his salvation was offered to me and from this time I resolve to give myself to him.' Lay this resolve on your conscience and remind yourself that if you go back from it then it is a token that you deserve to go to hell.

(ii)   Do not put this decision off to another time. This is as good a time as any. Something may happen before you have another opportunity; something may drive you further from Christ and make it much more difficult to come to him. Those who ignore the evil day and live in present pleasures and lusts have many things to satisfy them now. They do not say, 'There is no hope,' because they 'have found the life of their hand' (*Isa.* 57:10). But you have nothing in this world apart from Christ to bring comfort, joy and peace to your soul; neither will your end be any better than theirs if you die without Christ. So come to Christ now. He has waited a long time for you. Who knows how soon he may withdraw, never to come to you again?

It is unbelief working in the darkness of men's minds

and the obstinacy of their wills that effectually keeps sinners from coming to Christ, yet it covers itself in various guises so that it may not be seen in all its ugliness. For no sin is so horrible as this unbelief which is exposed in the clear light of the gospel. So, unbelief is helped by Satan's suggesting excuses to sinners so that they see nothing sinful in refusing to come to Christ (see *2 Cor.* 4:4). There may be many reasons why they do not come to Christ, but unbelief, in their eyes, is not one of them!

Objection

You tell us to come to Christ. Well, what would you have us do? We hear the Word preached, we believe it as well as we can. We do many things willingly. We make every effort to abstain from many evils. What more do you want us to do?

Answer

Those in the gospel who thought they had done their duty, and being pressed to believe by Jesus Christ asked him with some indignation, 'What shall we do, that we may work the works of God?' (*John* 6:28). If what we do is not enough, what more do you require from us? It was the same with the young man who asked, 'What do I still lack?' (*Matt.* 19:20). So do not be too confident of your state, lest you should yet lack that one thing. That lack may prove to be your eternal ruin.

You may have done nothing which contains even a spark of that faith which brings salvation. Simon Magus heard the Word, and believed as well as he could. Herod heard John the Baptist, and did many things gladly. And all kinds of hypocrites, when convicted of sin, do many duties and abstain from many sins. Yet, notwithstanding all this, they may still perish for ever.

These things can exist without faith, but faith cannot exist without them. There is a fundamental act of faith by which we receive Christ. This is the foundation of the Christian life. All other things belong to the building. This foundation faith is the one thing needed. Such faith is recognized by two particular properties.

The faith that receives Christ is unique. Jesus said, 'This is the work of God, that you believe in him whom he sent' (*John* 6:29). That faith which receives Christ is a unique work in which the soul gives special obedience to God. Therefore you must examine yourself to find out whether you have done that one thing required which is to receive Christ by faith for salvation.

This faith is accompanied with a spiritual change in the soul. 'Therefore, if anyone is in Christ, he is a new creation; old things have passed away; behold all things have become new' (*2 Cor.* 5:17). So if you do not choose to deceive yourself as to whether you have truly received Christ, then examine yourself. Have you been fundamentally changed?

Objection

But I do not know how to receive Christ by faith. I have tried to believe and cannot. So I have decided to do my best without receiving Christ. Frankly, I despair of ever being able to come to Christ by faith. It is not unbelief but this despair that keeps me from Christ.

Answer

Do you remember when the disciples had been fishing all night and had caught nothing (*Luke* 5:3-4)? Christ told them to go out and try again. Peter makes an excuse but does what Christ commands, and as a result caught an astonishing draught of fishes. So try again. Make every effort once again to receive him. You do not know what success he may give you.

Frankly, it is not your failure in trying to come to Christ, but your willingness to give up trying that will be your ruin. The woman of Canaan in her cries to Christ for mercy persisted though rebuffed three times (*Matt.* 15:22-28). Firstly, Christ did not respond to her cries. Then his disciples desired that he would send her away. Then Christ gave her two reasons why he should not answer her request. But still she does not give up. She goes on crying for mercy. Had she given up she would never have had the answer to her prayer. It may be you have prayed, and cried and promised, but all without success—as you suppose. Nevertheless, if you do not give up, you will win through in the end. You do not know when God will come to you with his grace. You do not know when Christ will reveal his love to you as he did to the poor woman in spite of his earlier rebuffs. As far as you know, he may enable you to receive Christ today. But if not, then he will enable you to receive him tomorrow or at some later day. Persevere! That is your duty. Do not give up in despair.

Take hold of this promise: 'Blessed is the man who listens to me, watching daily at my gates, waiting at the posts of my doors' (*Prov.* 8:34). If you hear him and wait, though you have not yet been admitted into his presence, but seem to be kept at the gate, in the end you will be blessed.

The rule to follow is this: 'Let us pursue the knowledge of the Lord.' If we do that, then, 'He will come to us like the rain, like the latter and former rain to the earth' (*Hos.* 6:3). Are you doing everything in your power to come to the knowledge of Christ? Even although you do not yet have any evidence that you have received him, nothing can ruin you but your giving up in despair. If you make every effort to know the Lord, then he will come to you like the rain. Many could tell you that if they had given up when overwhelmed with difficulties and disappointments, they would have been utterly ruined for ever. But now they are at rest and at peace in the bosom of Christ. Unable to accept Christ's teaching, many disciples 'went back and walked with him no more' (*John* 6:66). Christ lost many disciples, and they lost their souls. Beware, then, of letting discouragement persuade you to give up.

Objection

Yes, I admit I must come to Christ by faith or I am lost. But I cannot come now. There are many things I must do first. I do not have the time to spend trying to come to Christ. So I will wait until I have more time.

Answer

This is incontrovertible proof of the foolishness and deceitfulness of unbelief (*Tit.* 3:3). Can anything be more foolish than to put off considering the eternal destiny of your soul? To prefer present trifles (which will only lead to eternal misery) to eternal blessedness is the height of folly. You come to hear the Word, and when you go away, the language of your heart is, 'A little sleep, a little slumber, a little folding of the hands to sleep' (*Prov.* 6:10). Do you say, 'We will remain as we are for a little while longer, and then we will stir ourselves up to take hold of Christ for salvation'? Under this deceit, multitudes perish every day. This is a dark and evil disguise under which unbelief hides.

You need to realize that if you are putting off coming to

Christ and leaving it to a supposedly better time, you are under the power of Satan. He is likely to hold you fast and not let you go until he has brought you to eternal destruction.

Remember that the biblical promise of grace to enable you to receive Christ refers only to 'now', to this very day. 'Behold, *now* is the accepted time; behold, *now* is the day of salvation' (*2 Cor.* 6:3). It gives you no promise that you will be enabled to come to Christ on any other day. '*Today* if you will hear his voice, do not harden your hearts', is the Holy Spirit's word to you (*Heb.* 3:7). And again, 'But exhort one another daily, while it is called "Today", lest any of you be hardened through the deceitfulness of sin.' Beware of coming short of God's grace because you despised the day it was offered to you. Redeem the time or you are lost for ever.

As for making your present concerns and business an excuse for putting off Christ, why not receive him by faith? Then he will be your wisdom to guide and help you in all your concerns. 'One who is perfect in knowledge' will then be with you (*Job* 36:4).

Many put off receiving Christ because they do not wish to renounce their lusts and pleasures and perhaps have to face unpopularity also. Unlike Moses, they want to keep in with the pleasures of sin rather than suffer with the people of God.

The Jesuits preached and painted Christ among some of the Indians, but they did not tell them of his cross and sufferings. They told the Indians only of Christ's present glory and power. In this way they pretended to win them over to faith in Christ. But by hiding from them what might discourage them they preached a false Christ. We dare not do any such thing. Nor will we compromise with your lusts and sins. Cursed is the person who encourages you to come to Christ and allows you to think that you can still indulge one sin in your life.

I am not saying that when you come to Christ you will at once be absolutely and perfectly free from all sin. But in your heart and by a holy determination you must daily mortify all sin as grace enables you. Your choice of Christ must be wholehearted with no thought of turning back to some favourite sin. It is either God or the world, Christ or Satan, holiness or sin. They cannot be reconciled (*2 Cor.* 6:15-18).

As for your pleasures, the truth is, you have never yet known real pleasure and will not until you come to Christ. For only in Christ are true pleasures to be found. A few moments with Christ are to be preferred to an eternity with the cursed pleasures of this world (*Prov.* 3:13-18, *Ps.* 16:11).

Objection

But many believers do not seem to be any better than unbelievers! I am as good as those who claim to have received Christ! So why should I receive Christ?

Answer

Among true believers are many false and corrupt hypocrites. The tares look very like the wheat. Some whom we judge to be true believers, because of their unmortified pride, or covetousness, or careless unchristian behaviour, or their worldly dress and their conformity to the world, give rise to the sneers and jeers of the world. God is displeased with such believers. Christ and the gospel are dishonoured. Many who are weak in the faith are wounded and others are discouraged. But as for you, you are not told to come to Christ only if all Christians behave perfectly or are all better than you. Hypocrites will end up in hell and you will be with them if you do not receive Christ by faith. You are to put your faith in his Word which will never let you down. In any case, you—like other worldly people—do not know how, nor are you able, to make a right judgement of believers. Only the spiritual man is able to discern the things of God. The weaknesses of believers are visible to all, but graces are invisible. But when you are able to make a right judgement of true believers, you will desire above all things to be one of them (*Ps.* 16:3).

These few examples show us how unbelief covers its deformity and hides that destruction which it inevitably brings with it. But a little spiritual wisdom will tear off these disguises and expose it in all its hideous enmity against the glory of Christ.

16: *How to Recognize Spiritual Decay in the Soul*

Only a steady view of the glory of Christ by faith will graciously revive from inward spiritual declensions and decays and fill with fresh springs of grace, even in old age. This truth is confirmed by Scripture, and is the joyful experience of multitudes of believers.

There are two things that elderly Christians, who have for many long years believed and lived by faith in Christ, long for when they are nearing eternity. The first is, that all their spiritual backslidings will be healed and that they may be spiritually revived and recovered from all the spiritual declensions and decays to which they were liable in their daily walk with God. The other is, that they may flourish in holiness and fruitfulness to the praise of God, the honour of the gospel, and the increase of their own peace and joy. They value these things more than all the world. They cannot stop thinking about them and longing to experience more of them.

Those who have no interest in these things, whatever their claim to faith in Christ, are completely ignorant of their true condition. For it is the nature of grace to grow and increase to the end. Like rivers, the nearer they come to the ocean, the more is their water content increased, and they flow more swiftly. So will grace flow more freely and fully the nearer it approaches the ocean of eternal glory. Where this is not so, there is no saving grace.

Paul tells us that 'though our outward man is perishing,

yet the inward man is being renewed day by day' (*2 Cor.* 4:16). This is of great comfort in our old age. The weaker our physical bodies become, the greater is our spiritual renewal. This promise gives great strength to elderly believers.

In the holy and wise providence of God afflictions and troubles increase with age. That is especially true of ministers of the gospel. Many of them share Peter's lot: 'When you were younger, you girded yourself and walked where you wished; but when you are old, you will stretch out your hands, and another will gird you and carry you where you do not wish' (*John* 21:18).

Besides the physical ailments and pains which come with old age, the affairs of life also may weigh more heavily on older people, when they are looking forward to a quiet retirement, and are thinking with Job, 'I shall die in my nest' (*Job* 29:18). Jacob, for example, after all his hard labour to provide for his family, found great troubles in his old age. It almost broke his heart. Often both persecution and public dangers fall upon them at the same time. While the outward man is perishing, we need inward spiritual strength so that we will be able to persevere. And this can only happen as we experience daily spiritual renewals in the inner man. Exactly this is promised to us in Scripture.

Take, for example, the promises in Psalm 92:12-15. 'The righteous shall flourish like a palm tree. He shall grow like a cedar in Lebanon' (verse 12). This promise relates to the times of the Messiah for this is prophesied of him. 'In his days the righteous shall flourish' (*Ps.* 72:7). And how will they flourish? By the abundance of grace that he will pour on them out of his fullness (*John* 1:16, *Col.* 1:19). In this, and not in outward prosperity or external ornaments of divine worship, lies the glory of the gospel. The flourishing of the righteous in grace and holiness is the glory of the office of Christ and of the gospel. And where this does not happen, there is no glory in our claim to a true faith in Christ. Just as the glory of kings is in the wealth and peace of their subjects, so the glory of Christ is in the grace and holiness of his subjects.

This flourishing is compared to the palm tree, and to the cedar of Lebanon. The palm tree is green, beautiful and fruitful and the cedar is great, strong and of great age. So the righteous are compared to the palm tree for beauty of character and fruitfulness in obedience; to the cedar for continual, constant growth and increase in grace. But sinful, spiritual decay and backsliding make them more like shrubs and heaths in the desert rather than like the palm tree or the cedars of Lebanon.

'Those who are planted in the house of the Lord shall flourish in the courts of our God' (verse 13). This describes all the righteous; not just a few. They *flourish* because they are planted in the house of the Lord, that is, in the church. To be *planted* in the house of the Lord is to be fixed and rooted in the grace communicated by the ordinances of divine worship. Unless we are planted in the house of the Lord, we cannot flourish in his courts (see *Ps.* 1:3). Unless we are partakers of the grace administered in the ordinances we cannot flourish in a fruitful Christian life.

Hypocrites can participate outwardly in divine ordinances. They bear some leaves, but do not grow like the cedar, nor grow fruit like the palm tree. So Paul prays for believers, that Christ may dwell in their hearts by faith, that they may be 'rooted and grounded in love', and 'rooted, built up and established' (*Eph.* 3:17, *Col.* 2:7). This is why we have so many fruitless Christians. They have entered the courts of God by a profession of faith, but were never planted in his house by faith and love.

So do not deceive yourself. You may have become a member of the outward church and been made a partaker of its outward privileges, and yet not be so planted in it as to flourish in grace and fruitfulness.

But what is of supreme importance here is the grace and privilege the psalmist promises to old age. 'They shall still bear fruit in old age; they shall be fresh and flourishing' (verse 14). There are three things required for a 'fresh and flourishing' spiritual state.

(i) Believers should continually receive the heavenly, life-giving sap of the true olive of Christ himself (*Rom.* 11:17). This is the secret of the spiritual life and grace derived from him. When this abounds in them, keeping their spiritual life from withering, they are said to be 'fresh', which in Scripture means strong and healthy.

(ii) Believers should flourish and grow strong by feeding on the Word of God and so continue to present a glorious witness to the world.

(iii) Believers should still bring forth fruit in all holy obedience.

All these are promised to them in their old age.

Even trees, when they grow old, are apt to dry up and lose their greenness. Similarly, it is rare to see an old man naturally vigorous, healthy and strong, and it is also rare to see aged believers flourishing spiritually. But this is what is promised to all believers: to them will be given special grace beyond what can be illustrated by the growth and fruitfulness of plants and trees.

The grace meant is this: when believers are growing old and are experiencing bodily weaknesses and pain and may also be suffering spiritual decay, provision is made in the covenant to keep them fresh, flourishing and fruitful. They will be kept vigorous by the power of divine grace and fruitful in all duties of obedience. This is what we will now consider. But let us first bless God for this encouragement to believers in their old age that they will still continue to be fresh and flourishing.

The psalmist declares the greatness of this privilege. 'To declare that the Lord is upright; he is my rock, and there is no unrighteousness in him' (*Ps.* 92:15). Consider the difficulties that believers face in old age, the temptations that must be conquered, the increasing darkness and slowness of mind, the increasing physical tiredness, the cries of the flesh to be spared, and we shall see the faithfulness, power and righteousness of God in keeping his covenant promises. Nothing else could keep believers fresh and flourishing in their old age.

Having laid the foundation of this glorious testimony, I will now show that it is by a steady view of the glory of Christ in the gospel that believers are kept fresh and flourishing in their old age.

If a man has made a great profession of faith when he was young, and now in his old age he is dead, cold, worldly and selfish, if he has no fresh springs of spiritual life in him, it is clear that he has a barren heart that never was really fruitful to God. Many stand in need of being stirred up by such a warning to make every effort to find out where they stand spiritually.

There is often a late Spring in the year, a Spring in Autumn. It is faint and weak but useful to the farmer for it is a clear sign to him that if his ground is not barren it will flourish afresh towards the end of the year. So God, the good farmer, looks for the same from us, especially if we have had a summer drought in our lives (*Ps.* 32:4). True, the late spring does not produce the same fruit as does early spring; but it is evidence that the ground is in good heart and puts forth what is right for that time of year. It may be that the graces which were active in a person newly converted will not abound in the late spring of old age. But those graces which are right for that time of life will flourish, such as spirituality, heavenly mindedness, being weaned from the world and readiness for the cross and for death. These are necessary even in old age, to prove that we have a living power of grace and to show by this that God is indeed 'our rock, and there is no unrighteousness in him'.

Spiritual life has a power in it to grow and flourish to the end, unless neglected. True spiritual life is quite different from temporary faith. Temporary faith flourishes for a while and produces some fruit. But it does not abide, grow and flourish. After a while it withers and dies. Jesus described it in his parable of the sower (*Matt.* 13:20-21). Either some great trial extinguishes it, or it slowly withers, until the mind in which it was is left utterly barren. But true spiritual life grows and thrives to the end. Those who have it will still bring forth fruit in their old age.

Scripture compares spiritual life to those things that grow and thrive. 'But the path of the just is like the shining sun, that shines ever brighter to the perfect day' (*Prov.* 4:18). The morning light begins at dawn and shines more and more until noon. So is the spiritual life of the justified believer; it shines more and more until the perfect day of glory. On the other hand the light of temporary faith starts as the noonday sun but gets less and less until it ends in darkness. Where there is a saving principle of grace in the soul, it will grow and thrive to the end. If it is allowed to wither for a while, it gives no peace to the soul until it is flourishing once again. Peace in a spiritually withering condition is ruination to the soul giving it a sense of false security from which it is difficult to free it.

This spiritual life is also called by Christ 'living water', indeed, 'a well of water springing up into everlasting life' (*John* 4:10-14). It is a well continually supplied by a bubbling spring. It never dries up. So true believers in old age show more and more love, meekness, self-denial and spirituality. Whereas temporary faith dries up, producing the dust of pride, self-love and earthly mindedness.

Scripture gives many divine promises to believers that they will always be well supplied with grace so that their spiritual life will grow and flourish to the end. Psalm 92:12-15 which we have discussed is but one example. By these promises, we are made partakers of the divine nature (*2 Pet.* 1:4).

Isaiah also gives us such a promise: 'For I will pour water on him who is thirsty, and floods on the dry ground; I will pour my Spirit on your descendants, and my blessing on your offspring; they will spring up among the grass like willows by the watercourses' (*Is.* 44:3-4).

This promise concerns firstly the gracious way God dealt with his ancient people, the Jews, after their return from captivity. Yet it also refers to the redemption of the church by Jesus Christ which was illustrated by the deliverance of the Jews from captivity. It is chiefly fulfilled in the times of the gospel, when the righteous were to flourish and thrive. It is a promise of a new *covenant*; it is not only given to believers but also to their descendants and offspring, which is the sign of the new covenant promises.

In this promise we learn what we were before our conversion. We were thirsty, dry and barren ground. Left to ourselves we would wither and die. But God pours on us the sanctifying water of his Spirit and the blessing of his grace. We are converted and the result is a spiritual life that thrives and flourishes to the end.

The promises of the new covenant made to the elect, concerning the first work of grace, are absolutely free and unconditional. The first work of regeneration enabling the elect sinner to repent and believe is effected freely by grace alone and not because the elect have done anything to deserve it. The glory of covenant promises is that they infallibly assure the elect that God will carry out his immutable purposes and decrees. To the elect these promises infallibly bring about conversion and sanctification and are bestowed on them absolutely freely and unconditionally.

But the promises concerning *the growth* of this grace in believers are not unconditional. According to 2 Peter 1:4-10, many duties are required so that these promises might be fulfilled and accomplished in us. Believers are expected to make every effort to grow strong in grace. God does indeed sometimes work sovereignly, bestowing healing grace on backsliding believers (e.g. *Isa.* 57:17-18). Many a poor soul has thus been delivered from going down into the pit. The good shepherd will go out of his way to save a wandering sheep. But we must not presume on God's goodness by neglecting the duties we are called to fulfil.

So, notwithstanding these gracious promises, if we neglect to do those things which enable grace to flourish and grow, our spiritual life will begin to wither and weak–en. Fervent prayer, responding to the grace we receive and being careful to carry out our biblical duties are necessary to keep grace flourishing and strong.

God has provided food so that our spiritual life might grow, be strengthened and flourish. Life is sustained by food, and the food provided for our souls is the Word of God and all other ordinances of divine worship (*1 Pet.* 2:2-3). If we do not eat our daily food, our bodies will soon grow weak and lifeless. If believers do not feed daily on God's Word and the divine ordinances, then it is no wonder their spiritual life begins to wither. But God has provided for our spiritual growth and prosperity even in old age.

So we see that there is a power in spiritual life that enables it to thrive, grow and flourish right to the end of our lives. Although God has provided for the growth of spiritual life in believers, it is still subject to decline and decay which causes anxiety and threatens eternal ruin.

Spiritual decays are of two kinds. There are those decays which are brought about gradually, and those which are brought about by sudden, unexpected temptations, catching the soul by surprise, withering its spiritual powers and depriving it of all solid peace.

As for temporary believers, give them enough time in this world, especially if they experience outward prosperity or persecution, and their hypocrisy will soon be seen by all. Though they may keep up a form of godliness, yet they deny the power of it in their lives (*Prov.* 1:31, *2 Tim.* 3:5). Even if they do not openly abandon all religious duties, yet these will grow so lifeless and tasteless that their hypocrisy will be evident to everyone. This is the state of those who are lukewarm, neither hot nor cold, who have the reputation of being alive, but are dead.

The difference between temporary believers and true believers is that temporary believers are not aware that they are backsliding because their minds are taken up with other things. Or if they feel they are not as keenly religious as they once were, they are not too concerned about it. If they begin to feel guilty they say, 'A little sleep, a little slumber, a little folding of the hands to sleep' (*Prov.* 6:10). But when true believers find their spiritual life is withering and they are backsliding, they become restless and begin to seek revival. True believers cannot rest happily in such a state.

Gradual spiritual decay is seen in five of the seven churches of Asia (*Rev.* 2-3). Some of them, such as Sardis and Laodicea, were in great danger of utter rejection. These churches are examples of such decays in all churches and all believers in the world. And those who do not think themselves liable to spiritual decays are dead in sin, and use all means to cover up their miserable condition and appear to be flourishing in the eyes of the world.

This is how the church of Rome deceives the world, and I wish other churches would not follow her example.

Spiritual decays brought about by sudden and unexpected temptations, produce spiritual distress at being under God's displeasure.

David describes this condition in Psalm 38:1-10. He is in a terrible state. Knowing he was called of God to be a teacher and instructor of the church in all ages, he records his experience for her edification. So the title of the psalm is 'To bring to remembrance'. Some think that David was talking about some great disease from which he was suffering. But if this is so, it would only be the immediate reason for his complaint. The actual cause of his disease was sin alone.

David tells us four things about himself:

(i) He had departed from God and had fallen into great sins. This had produced great mental distress (verses 3-4).

(ii) He had foolishly continued in these sins and had not sought healing grace and mercy. So his condition had grown worse (verse 5). This is what makes such a condition dangerous: if when we have been unexpectedly and suddenly surprised by sin, we do not quickly go to Christ for healing.

(iii) He tells us that he had a continual awareness of God's displeasure (verses 2-4).

(iv) He describes how he was restless in this state, mourning, groaning and making every effort to be delivered (verses 6-10).

Only those who have experienced them know the pain of a soul convinced of such spiritual decays. It casts us down to the earth. We go mourning all day alone; others know nothing of our sorrows. But how sad to see professing Christians revealing their inward decays by their outward fruits, yet not the slightest bit concerned about it! The former are heading for revival, but the latter are in the pathway leading to death.

Gradual decline in the life and power of grace arises from formality in holy duties, persistent involvement in the affairs of this life, an over-valuation of sinful enjoyments, growth and worldly wisdom, neglect of daily mortification of sins, with the secret influence of the temptation to think we can do something because everyone else does it.

Many who profess the Christian faith fall into spiritual decline and do not experience the power of God's promises of fruitfulness. This state does not glorify Christ, nor does it bring honour to the gospel. Anyone who is in this state is in great spiritual danger. Few in this state come to Christ for healing. If people do not realise they are sick, they will not seek a cure. And some who realize they are sick do not use the right cure (see *Hos.* 5:13).

The following questions will help to convict us if we suffer from such spiritual sickness:

Have you in your Christian life had any experience of spiritual declensions? No doubt there are some who have always flourished spiritually, and who have never fallen under the power of laziness, neglect or temptation, at least not for a long time. But they are few. Scarcely any Old Testament believer was free from spiritual decay and decline. Some, like David, sank into terrible spiritual decay, but were wonderfully delivered. Notice how he praises God for healing his backslidings (*Ps.* 103:1, 3-5). There is no grace that fills the hearts of believers with more gratitude and joy, than being delivered from backsliding. When the soul is brought out of prison, then it is filled with praise (*Ps.* 142:7). So I ask, have you experienced such spiritual decline in your life? If you have not, then I fear it is for one of the following reasons.

Reason One
You probably have never had any flourishing, spiritual state in your soul. Someone who has always been weak and sickly does not know what it means to be healthy and strong because he has never experienced it. But those who know what it is to be healthy and then fall sick, know the difference. They know when they are sick!

Many who make an outward profession live in all sorts of sins. But if you challenge their backsliding, you will seem to them as Lot did to his sons-in-law, when he told them of the impending destruction of Sodom. They thought he was playing a joke on them (*Gen.* 19:14). They have always been as they are. They have never been any different; it is 'ridiculous' to speak to them of the need to be revived.

So we must be able to say, 'Remember therefore from where you have fallen; repent and do the first works' (*Rev.* 2:5). They must have experienced a better state, or they would not make every effort to be revived. So those who see no evil or danger in their present backsliding state, but think that all is well enough with them, because they are as good as ever they were, will not easily be brought to admit their need of revival. These people need to ask themselves whether they have been truly born again of God's Spirit.

If you have not experienced any backsliding or spiritual declensions, then it is to be feared that you are asleep in a false security, which is hardly distinguishable from death in sin. The church of Laodicea had declined from her first faith and obedience. Yet she felt secure in her condition. She had so little insight into her backslidden state that she saw herself as a thriving, flourishing church. She thought she was rich, that is, in gifts and graces; but in reality she was 'wretched, and miserable, and poor, and blind and naked' (*Rev.* 3:17). So is it with many churches today, especially those who boast that they are without error or blame. It is strange that a church should think that it is rich in graces and gifts, when in reality it is nothing but a clanging cymbal.

God said, concerning Ephraim, that 'grey hairs are here and there on him, yet he does not know it' (*Hos.* 7:9). He was in a declining, dying condition, but did not realize it: 'They do not return to the Lord their God, nor seek him for all this' (verse 10). If we will not recognize and admit our spiritual decline, then there is no hope of persuading us to return to the Lord. 'The healthy have no need of a physician, but the sick.' Christ did not 'come to call the righteous, but sinners to repentance'. Such people are under the power of a stupefying false sense of security. This is why we have so little success in calling such persons to experience revival in their souls.

Reason Two
You may have never experienced true spiritual peace and joy in your soul. Scripture testifies that true faith produces

joy and peace. So have you experienced such peace and joy? Have you, in trials and sudden unexpected temptations or calamities been quickly calmed by them? Or are you easily disturbed, anxious and troubled? A declining spiritual state and solid spiritual peace cannot exist together. So by the lack of spiritual joy and peace you may know your true condition.

How much does pride, selfishness, worldliness in thought and dress and corrupt immoral talk play in your life? How difficult it sometimes is to tell the difference between Christians and worldly people in their outward appearance and in matters of behaviour and conversation! Many who say they are followers of Christ are so conformed to the world that their witness counts for nothing.

God says of many of us, what he said of his ancient people the Jews, 'You have been weary of me, O Israel' (*Isa.* 43:22). Have we been weary of God, when really we ought to be weary with ourselves? But how have we shown our weariness of God? Have we not been faithful in all religious duties? What more must we do?

It is possible to weary God by the way we fulfil our spiritual responsibilities (*Isa.* 1:13-14). As the prophet Malachi said, 'You have wearied the Lord with your words' (2:17). God says he is weary with everything you do for him, and you say you are weary with everything you do for God (*Mal.* 1:13). You think you are being faithful to God but that he does not reward you as he should. You find no joy in your religion. You have given up holding regular family prayers, or they are only done sporadically and formally. Although family prayer is grounded in the light of nature and shows the family is dedicated to God, and is encouraged by the example of all the saints of old, and necessary in the experience of all that walk with God, yet you make excuses and justify yourself in your neglect of this duty. You show your weariness also by neglecting attendance at public worship. You used to find public worship a joy, but now, what a weariness it is! Things show that you are indeed getting fed up with God and with the things of God.

But this is not what I mean. Men may be weary of God while they yet still happily observe a multitude of outward duties. Men may draw near to God with their lips when their hearts are far from him. God is Spirit, and he will be worshipped in spirit and in truth. Such worship cannot exist without the graces of his Spirit in his worshippers, for 'bodily exercise profits a little, but godliness is profitable for all things' (1 Tim. 4:8).

So if you are to avoid growing weary of God and with the things of God then you must continually stir up all the graces of the Spirit in you as you seek spiritual revival in your soul. Do not plunge straight into prayer or worship, but spend time meditating on the glory of Christ first and in this way the graces necessary for carrying out that duty will be roused and ready. Keep a prayerful watch for those temptations that will try and draw you away from this holy duty. Many excuses will arise to persuade you to put off the duty of reviving your spiritual life. Laziness, formality, physical tiredness and the business of life will combine to frustrate every effort you make.

The outward performance of religious duties, be they never so many, or however strictly they are imposed, is an easy task. It demands less hard work than men put into their various trades and callings. And in performing their religious duties, either in public or in their families, men may be weary of God. And the more unspiritual they are the greater their weariness. So we can measure ourselves by this: Are we weary of God and the duties he calls us to? But if you constantly stir yourself up to take hold of God, it is proof that your soul is in good spiritual health (*Isa.* 64:7). But this will not be done without the utmost watchfulness and care against the desires of the flesh and other temptations.

Many who are outwardly faithful still allow themselves to continue to indulge a known sin. Faithfulness in such external duties has no power to mortify sin. Indeed we may keep up a form of godliness to cover up the absence of its power. Indeed, where any known sin is indulged and no effort is made to mortify it, and where our religious duties are not used, applied and directed to the putting to death of sin and the flourishing of spiritual life, we will soon get weary of them and of God.

Examine yourself concerning those graces which tend most to glorify God. Zeal, humility, contriteness of heart, spiritual mindedness, strength of soul, delight in God's ways, love, self-denial and similar graces are those which tend most to glorify God and these you must make every effort to cultivate in your soul. So ask yourself whether your soul is fresh and flourishing in these graces. Are they in you? Do they abound? (see *2 Pet.* 1:8).

The loss of a spiritual appetite for the food of our souls is proof that our graces have withered and declined. Peter says, 'As newborn babes, desire the pure milk of the word, that you may grow thereby, if indeed you have tasted that the Lord is gracious' (*1 Pet.* 2:2-3). Spiritual life shows itself in a healthy appetite for the Word, grounded on an experience of God's grace in it. How healthy then is your spiritual appetite? If you have no appetite for God's Word then your spiritual life is in a bad state.

When men grow old they lose much of the natural appetite. They must continue to eat to maintain life, but they do not have such a hearty appetite as they did in their younger days. So they begin to criticize the food or the cooking. But the change is in themselves. Elderly believers may complain that the preaching they hear now is not so fine as what they heard when they were younger. But the change may actually be in themselves. They have lost their spiritual appetite and do not hunger and thirst for heavenly food as they once did.

'A satisfied soul loathes the honeycomb, but to a hungry soul every bitter thing is sweet' (*Prov.* 27:7). Men, filled with pride, boasting of their abilities, have lost their spiritual appetite for God's Word, and this makes the Word lose its power and effectiveness to them. That Word which David says is 'sweeter than honey and the honeycomb', has little or no taste or relish in it for them. If they were spiritually hungry, the most bitter reproofs would be sweet. They come to hear the Word with a weak spiritual appetite, not expecting to receive much from the preaching, as if they were invited to a feast after they had already eaten. This loss of spiritual appetite is a sure proof of spiritual decay in the soul.

Not making Christ and his service the main business of our lives is another evidence of spiritual decay in the soul. Where grace is flourishing in the soul then all other things will be secondary to the duties of Christ's religion. Everything else must take second place. Christ must have first place in every area of life. If men devote themselves to the affairs of the world, being ruled and controlled by worldly concerns, only occasionally patronizing Christ's service, it is foolish to say that following him is their chief business. But the greatest evidence of spiritual decay in the soul is when serving Christ is no longer the chief business in life. Examine your spiritual state in the light of this. What place does Christ's service play in your life? Is it your chief joy? Or do you only patronize it occasionally?

A low spiritual state shows itself in a lack of love to the saints, barrenness in good works and an unreadiness and unwillingness to respond to the calls of God to repent and reform. These are all undeniable evidences that those in whom they are found either have no true grace at all, or have fallen into serious spiritual decay in their souls. But thank God that one can recover from such spiritual decay. This is the subject of our next chapter.

17: *How the Soul may be Recovered from Spiritual Decays*

A believer who has allowed his spiritual life to wither and decay may recover and be revived, provided he goes about it the right way. If every time we slip back on our climb to the heights of heaven, we cannot be recovered, then we would all surely perish. If salvation were only for those who never slipped back then none would be in heaven. If the Lord should mark iniquities, who could stand? (*Ps.* 130:3).

When a tree grows old, or is decaying, it helps to loosen the soil around its base and then to manure it. This may revive it and cause it to flourish again. But if you uproot it and plant it somewhere else—which may appear to be a good thing to do—it will probably wither and die. This is exactly what some spiritual backsliders have done. Finding themselves growing more and more unspiritual, they leave their own church and go over to Rome or to some other denomination, thinking that the fault lies with the teaching of the church they are in, when in reality the fault lies in themselves. Such people have visibly withered and died spiritually. But if they had used the right means for healing and recovery, they might have flourished and brought forth much fruit.

To recover and be revived we need to mortify our sins and lusts and make every effort to carry out the spiritual duties God requires. Mortification is a means to revive spiritual life. But it must be done scripturally, by the help of the Holy Spirit (*Rom.* 8:13). All other ways of putting to death our sins and lusts are condemned by God who asks, 'Who has required these things at your hands?'. Like the Pharisees, Roman Catholicism brought the duty of spiritual mortification of sin into disrepute. They invented works, ways and duties which God never appointed, which he will never accept and which can never benefit men's souls. Examples are: confession to a priest, various disciplines, pilgrimages, fastings, abstinence and set prayers to be repeated in stated canonical hours. But no amount of external exercise in these things brings any spiritual benefit whatever.

But it is natural to turn to such helps in order to revive the soul. Those who are keenly aware of their sad spiritual state are burdened with a sense of guilt, for they know that it is sin that is responsible for their low spirituality. So the first question that arises is, how they may atone for that sin which has brought on them the divine displeasure and how they may once again be accepted by God. If they have no true evangelical light, two things immediately occur to them. First, some special course of duties, which God has not commanded. This is the way the church of Rome takes, and which guilt, in the darkness of corrupted nature, clamours for. Secondly, an extraordinary multiplication of duties, which for the most part are required of us. Micah gives us an example of both kinds (*Mic.* 6:6-7). In this way people hope to be restored to their previous flourishing spiritual state.

Awareness of spiritual decays is of two kinds. First, there is an awareness brought about by the power of convictions only, which are multiplied among temporary believers.

Secondly, there is an awareness brought about by a weakening of the power of saving grace in the soul. Those who are under convictions only, who are temporary believers, will turn for help to those man-made duties and works such as are devised by the church of Rome. When they fail, for the most part they stop wrestling with their sin and corruption and abandon themselves to the power of their lusts, for they have no evangelical light to guide them into the right way.

Those who are aware of a weakening of their experience of grace themselves must redouble their efforts in the duties of mortification and spiritual obedience, but take care that *what you do* is what God has appointed, and that *how you do it* is guided and directed by Scripture. Examples of such duties are the reading and hearing of the Word, fervent prayer and diligently guarding against all temptations to sin. There should be a special effort to keep the mind spiritual and heavenly. This will demand holy earnestness, and a strong resistance to any other attitude of mind.

But do not try these things in your own strength. The Holy Spirit rejects self-confidence (*2 Cor.* 3:5; 9:8). Self-confidence and self-sufficiency ignore Christ who alone is the Lord who heals us (*Exod.* 15:26). Another evil arises from self-confidence, when we do religious duties to build up merit and gain favour with God. No, what we do must be done by faith. Faith must seek Christ's help and his grace both for mortification and obedience, or they will not be of any help in our healing and recovery.

So the work of recovering backsliders or believers from spiritual decays is an act of sovereign grace, wrought in us by virtue of God's faithfulness to his divine promises. Because believers are liable to such declensions, backslidings and decays, God has given us great and precious promises that we will be recovered if we use the right means to such recovery. Scripture gives us an example of such a promise in Hosea 14:1-8. God speaks to Israel: 'O Israel, return to the Lord' (verse 1). This call was made when the generality of the people were wicked and were heading for destruction (see *Hos.* 13:16). So there is no time or situation which can prevent sovereign grace doing what it has purposed to do. It can work even in the midst of terrible judgements.

In such a time the true Israel of God, the elect themselves, are apt to be swamped by the sins of the whole nation, and so begin to backslide from God and to fall into spiritual declensions. This is what had happened to Israel, though she had not absolutely broken the covenant with God. He was still to her 'the Lord your God' (verse 1). Yet she had fallen in her iniquity. Times of public apostasy are often accompanied with partial spiritual decays (*Matt.* 24:12).

When God purposes graciously to heal the backsliding of his people he not only calls them to repentance, but also enables them to repent and gives them the desire to use the means of healing. This is what he does here. 'Take words with you, and return to the Lord' (verse 2). And this is what ministers must do when pressing on their congregations the duty of repentance. Tell them what they have to pray for.

The pathway to spiritual recovery is renewed repentance seen in the following:

Renewed repentance is seen in fervent prayer. 'Take words with you. Say to him . . .' We must know what we are to pray for. We are to pray for pardon of all iniquity. 'Take away all iniquity.' Not one sin must be left to be indulged. We are to pray that God will graciously receive us. 'Receive us graciously.' Confession must be made of the sins that caused our backslidings. 'Assyria will not save us. Nor will we say any more to the work of our hands, "You are our gods."' Fleshly confidence and false worship were the two great sins that ruined the people, and of these sins God expects a full and free confession so that we may be healed.

Believers must renew their covenant with God, renouncing all other hopes and expectations, and put their trust and confidence only and wholly in him, for only in God do the fatherless find mercy (verse 3). The result of such repentance is praise and thanksgiving: 'We will offer the sacrifice of our lips' (verse 2). When God heals our backslidings he will communicate his grace to us, to the praise of his own glory.

Unless we find these things wrought in us in such a way that prepares us to receive the mercy desired, we have no firm ground to expect to be made partakers of that mercy, for this is how God deals with the church. Only when serious repentance shows itself in fervent prayer, confession of sin and a renewed covenant with God as seen above, will God graciously receive us and revive us from all our spiritual decays. This grace will not suddenly be poured on us in our state of laziness, negligence and false assurance, but will stir us up to renew our repentance.

The work of grace in reviving us is seen in verses 4-8.

The purpose of this work is to heal our backsliding (verse 4, *Exod.* 15:26). This healing includes the forgiveness of sins, and a renewed supply of grace to make us fruitful in obedience. 'I will be like the dew to Israel.' This is how God heals the backslidings of believers.

God was moved simply by love to do this work of grace. 'I will love them freely' (verse 4). The actual means by which we are recovered is pardoning mercy. 'For my anger is turned away from him' (verse 4). And the means to restoring us to renewed obedience is a plentiful supply of effectual grace. 'I will be like the dew to Israel' (verse 5). The dew refers to the Spirit of grace who above all things is necessary to our healing and recovery. The healing of our backsliding and the restoration of our spiritual life to a thriving and flourishing state leads to abundant fruitfulness in holiness and obedience, in peace and love that had never been attained previously (verses 4-7).

It only remains to show the unique way by which, through faith, we may obtain this promise, namely, of being flourishing and fruitful even in old age.

(i) The first thing we need to know is that all our supplies of grace are from Jesus Christ. Grace is declared in the promises of the Old Testament, but how it is communicated to us and how we receive it is revealed to us in the New: all grace is from Christ. He has told us that 'without him, we can do nothing'. We can no more bear fruit than a branch separated from the vine (*John* 15:3-5). He is our head and all divine communications of grace are from him alone. He is our life and lives in us, so that all our strength for holiness and obedience comes from him (*Gal.* 2:20, *Col.* 3:1-4). So if we are in a low spiritual state and desire to be revived, we must look to Christ alone. Without Christ, everything else we do is nothing and will produce nothing.

(ii) The only way to receive supplies of spiritual strength and grace from Jesus Christ is by faith. We come to him, are grafted into him, and must abide in him by faith to bring forth fruit. He dwells in our hearts by faith. He works in us by faith and we live by faith in the Son of God. So if we receive anything from Christ we must receive it by faith. Scripture gives us no warrant to believe that we can receive anything from him except by faith.

(iii) The third thing we need to know is that this faith concerns the person of Christ, his grace, his whole mediatory work, with all its results, and his glory in them all. Therefore the one thing most needed in our recovery and revival is a steady view of the glory of Christ, in his person, grace and office through faith, or a constant, lively exercise of faith in him as he is revealed to us in Scripture. This is the only way to be revived and to receive such grace as will keep us fresh and flourishing even in old age. He that lives by faith in Christ shall, by his spiritual thriving and growth, 'declare that the Lord is upright; He is my rock, and there is no unrighteousness in Him.'

Scripture says, 'They looked to him and were radiant, and their faces were not ashamed' (*Ps.* 34:5). 'Look to me and be saved, all the ends of the earth' (*Isa.* 45:22). On this look to Christ, on this view of his glory, depends all our salvation. Therefore everything we need for our complete salvation is also communicated to us as we look to him. 'Therefore I will look to the Lord; I will wait for the God of my salvation' (see also *Zech.* 12:10, *Heb.* 12:2).

(iv) A constant view of the glory of Christ will revive our souls and cause our spiritual lives to flourish and thrive. Our souls will be revived by the transforming power with which beholding Christ is always accompanied. This is what transforms us daily into the likeness of Christ. So let us live in constant contemplation of the glory of Christ, and power will then flow from him to us, healing all our declensions, renewing a right spirit in us and enabling us to abound in all the duties that God requires of us.

Faith will fix our souls in Christ who will fill us with delight and satisfaction. This, in heaven, is perfect blessedness, for it is caused by the eternal vision of the glory of God in Christ. So the more we behold the glory of Christ by faith now, the more spiritual and the more heavenly will be the state of our souls.

The reason why the spiritual life in our souls decays and withers is because we fill our minds full of other things, and these things weaken the power of grace. But when the mind is filled with thoughts of Christ and his glory, these things will be expelled (see *Col.* 3:1-5, *Eph.* 5:8).

When we behold the glory of Christ by faith every grace in us will be stirred up. This is how our spiritual life is revived (see *Rom.* 5:3-5, *2 Pet.* 1:5-8).

All these thriving, flourishing graces in us will then make us more watchful against the deceitful workings of sin, temptations, foolish attitudes of mind and the vain thoughts which are the causes of our spiritual decays. Thus we will be able to behold the glory of Christ more clearly by faith in this world, and so prepare to behold the glory of Christ by sight in the next.

Then our Lord's prayer for us will be fully answered:

'Father, I desire that they also whom you gave me may be with me where I am, that they may behold my glory which you have given me; for you loved me before the foundation of the world' (*John* 17:24).

SOME OTHER
BANNER OF TRUTH
TITLES

THE WORKS OF JOHN OWEN

No outline can adequately summarise the significance of the life and work of John Owen (1616–1683). Summoned to preach before Parliament on several occasions, he was still only thirty-three when he addressed them on the day following the execution of King Charles I. A chaplain and adviser to Oliver Cromwell, he fell from the Protector's favour when he opposed the move to make him king. Even after the Great Ejection in 1662, he continued to enjoy some influence with Charles II who occasionally gave him money to distribute to impoverished ejected ministers. He was one of the leading Dissenters of his time.

It is, however, as an author that Owen is best known. During his lifetime he published over sixty titles of varying lengths; a dozen more appeared posthumously. Together they compose the twenty-four volume edition of his *Works* edited so ably by W. H. Goold in the mid-nineteenth century.

Owen's theology is marked by prodigious learning, profound thought and acute analysis of the human heart. Andrew Thomson, one of his biographers, says that Owen 'makes you feel when he has reached the end of his subject, that he has also exhausted it'. Both his subject matter – the great central themes of the Christian gospel – and his treatment of it – rich and satisfying, biblical and health-giving – secure him a permanent place in the galaxy of authors whose works deserve to be available for Christians in every age.

Owen's *Works* (with the exception of the one volume written in Latin) are published by the Banner of Truth Trust and are available as a set or in individual volumes. Contents of the twenty-three volumes are detailed overleaf.

CONTENTS OF THE TWENTY-THREE VOLUMES

DIVISION I: DOCTRINAL

VOLUME I

Life of Owen, by Andrew Thomson.
On the Person of Christ.
Meditations and Discourses on the Glory of Christ.
Meditations and Discourses on the Glory of Christ applied to
   Sinners and Saints.
Two Short Catechisms.

VOLUME 2

On Communion with God.
Vindication of the Preceding Discourse.
Vindication of the Doctrine of the Trinity.

VOLUME 3

Discourse on the Holy Spirit: His Name, Nature, Personality,
   Dispensation, Operations, and Effect – His Work in the Old
   and New Creation explained, and the Doctrines Vindicated.
The Nature and Necessity of Gospel Holiness; the difference
   between Grace and Morality, or a Spiritual Life Unto God in
   Evangelical Obedience, and a course of Moral Virtues, stated
   and declared.

VOLUME 4

The Reason of Faith.
Causes, Ways, and Means, of understanding the Mind of God, as
   revealed in His Word, with assurance therein. And a declaration of the perspicuity of the Scriptures, with the external
   means of the interpretation of them.
On the Work of the Holy Spirit in Prayer; with a brief inquiry into
   the nature and use of Mental Prayer and forms.
Of the Holy Spirit and His Work, as a Comforter and as the
   Author of Spiritual Gifts.

VOLUME 5

The Doctrine of Justification by Faith.
Evidences of the Faith of God's Elect.

DIVISION 2: PRACTICAL

VOLUME 6

On the Mortification of Sin.
On Temptation.
On Indwelling Sin in Believers.
Exposition of Psalm 130.

VOLUME 7

On the Nature and Causes of Apostasy, and the Punishment of
    Apostates.
On Spiritual-Mindedness.
On the Dominion of Sin and Grace.

VOLUME 8

Sermons.

VOLUME 9

Posthumous Sermons.

DIVISION 3: CONTROVERSIAL

VOLUME 10

A Display of Arminianism.
The Death of Death in the Death of Christ.
Of the Death of Christ.
A Dissertation on Divine Justice.

VOLUME 11

The Doctrine of the Saints' Perseverance Explained and Con-
    firmed.

VOLUME 12

Vindiciæ Evangelicæ: or, the Mystery of the Gospel Vindicated and Socinianism Examined.
Of the Death of Christ, and of Justification.
A Review of the Annotations of Grotius.

VOLUME 13

The Duty of Pastors and People Distinguished.
Eshcol: a Cluster of the Fruit of Canaan.
Of Schism; in Three Books.
Nonconformity Vindicated.
Tracts on the Power of the Magistrate, Indulgence, Toleration, etc.

VOLUME 14

Animadversions on 'Fiat Lux'.
Vindications of Animadversions.
The Church of Rome no safe Guide.
On Union among Protestants.
The State and Fate of Protestantism.

VOLUME 15

Discourse concerning liturgies.
Discourse concerning Evangelical Love, Church Peace, and Unity.
Inquiry concerning Evangelical Churches.
Answer to Dr. Stillingfleet on the unreasonableness of Separation.
Instruction in the Worship of God.

VOLUME 16

True Nature of a Gospel Church.
Tracts on Excommunication, Church Censures, Baptism, etc.
On the Divine Original of the Scriptures.
Posthumous Sermons.
Indices.

DIVISION 4: EXPOSITORY

VOLUME 17

Concerning the Epistle to the Hebrews.
Concerning the Messiah.
Concerning the Jewish Church.

VOLUME 18

The Sacerdotal Office of Christ.
A Day of Sacred Rest.
Summary of Observations on Hebrews.

VOLUME 19

Exposition of Hebrews, 1:1–3:6.

VOLUME 20

Exposition of Hebrews, 3:7–5:14.

VOLUME 21

Exposition of Hebrews, 6:1–7:28.

VOLUME 22

Exposition of Hebrews, 8:1–10:39.

VOLUME 23

Exposition of Hebrews, 11:1–13:25.

THE DEATH OF DEATH
IN THE DEATH OF CHRIST

John Owen
with an introduction by J. I. Packer

'*The Death of Death in the Death of Christ* is a polemical work, designed to show, among other things, that the doctrine of universal redemption is unscriptural and destructive of the gospel. Those who see no need for doctrinal exactness and have no time for theological debates which show up divisions between Evangelicals may well regret its reappearance. Some may find the very sound of Owen's thesis so shocking that they will refuse to read his book at all. But there are signs today of a new upsurge of interest in the theology of the Bible: a new readiness to test tradition, to search the Scriptures and to think through the faith. It is to those who share this readiness that Owen's treatise is offered, in the belief that it will help us in one of the most urgent tasks facing Evangelical Christendom today – the recovery of the gospel.

'It is safe to say that no comparable exposition of the work of redemption as planned and executed by the Triune Jehovah has ever been done since Owen published his. None has been needed.'

From the Introduction

The Death of Death appears in Volume 10 of the *Works of John Owen*.

ISBN 0 85151 382 4
316pp. Large paperback.

JOHN OWEN ON THE CHRISTIAN LIFE

Sinclair B. Ferguson

John Owen has long been recognised by evangelicals as one of the greatest of all English-speaking theologians. Several of his works have become theological classics. Like Augustine, whom he so admired, Owen's thinking touched both the depths of sin and the heights of grace. Many of his readers have come away from reading him on such themes as temptation, or indwelling sin, feeling that Owen knew them through and through.

The truth is that Owen had come – by intensive and constant study of both Scripture and the human heart – to know both himself and God. It was out of this rich experience that he preached and wrote on the loftiest themes of Christian theology.

Because of this background, Owen's teaching was always pastoral in its concern. His aim, said his assistant David Clarkson, was 'to promote holiness'. Consequently his work has survived through the centuries and is now more widely recognised and appreciated than it has been for many years. His writings address the fundamental issues Christians face in every age: How can I live the Christian life? How am I to deal with sin and temptation? How can I find assurance, and live for the honour of Jesus Christ?

John Owen on the Christian Life expounds Owen's teaching on these and related themes. The first book-length study of any aspect of Owen's thought, it also stands on its own as a study in pastoral theology. Ministers, Christian leaders, readers of Owen, and those who are daunted by the sheer voluminousness of his writings will find this book an ideal companion.

Dr Sinclair B. Ferguson is a member of the Faculty of Westminster Theological Seminary, Philadelphia, U.S.A.

ISBN 0 85151 503 7
316pp. Cloth-bound

APOSTASY FROM THE GOSPEL

Few subjects have received less attention from contemporary Christian writers than that of apostasy. The idea that professing Christians may prove not to be true Christians is, in many respects, too serious a prospect for our facile age. But, for John Owen, such avoidance of the issue was itself a pressing reason for writing on it at length and in great depth of spiritual analysis. His exposition is a masterpiece of penetration and discernment.

Now, in this modernised abridgement of Owen's work, Dr R.J.K. Law makes its powerful teaching readily accessible to modern readers. Some will find its pages deeply soul-searching; others will be struck by the clarity of Owen's insight; all will find a work which wounds in order to heal.

John Owen (1616–1683) was a leading Puritan pastor and theologian who served as a chaplain to Oliver Cromwell and later as Dean of Christ Church in the University of Oxford.

R.J.K. Law qualified as a medical doctor at St Thomas' Hospital but later entered the Anglican ministry. He ministers in four parishes in Devon and is married with four children.

ISBN 0 85151 609 2
184pp. Paperback

COMMUNION WITH GOD

John Owen (1616–83) believed that communion with God lies at the heart of the Christian life. With Paul he recognised that through the Son we have access by the Spirit to the Father. He never lost the sense of amazement expressed by John: 'Our fellowship is with the Father and with his Son, Jesus Christ.' In this outstanding book he explains the nature of this communion and describes the many privileges it brings.

Communion With God was written in a day, like our own, when the doctrine of the Trinity was under attack and the Christian faith was being reduced either to rationalism on the one hand or mysticism on the other. His exposition shows that nothing is more vital to spiritual well-being than a practical knowledge of what this doctrine means.

Until now, *Communion With God* has been read by only small numbers of Christians with access to the 275 closely printed pages in *The Works of John Owen*. Now Dr R. J. K. Law has produced a splendidly readable abridgement which brings Owen's rich teaching to a much wider readership.

Here is one of the greatest Christian classics of all time in a new format and more easily readable style.

ISBN 0 85151 607 6
224pp. Paperback

ALL THINGS FOR GOOD

Thomas Watson

Thomas Watson of St Stephen's, Walbrook believed he faced two great difficulties in his pastoral ministry. The first was making the unbeliever sad, in the recognition of his need of God's grace. The second was making the believer joyful, in response to God's grace. He believed the answer to the second difficulty could be found in Paul's teaching in Romans 8.28: God works all things together for good for his people.

First published in 1663 (under the title, *A Divine Cordial*), the year after Watson and some two thousand other ministers were ejected from the Church of England and exposed to hardship and suffering, *All Things For Good* contains the rich exposition of a man who lived in days when only faith in God's Word could lead him to such confidence.

Thomas Watson's exposition is always simple, illuminating and rich in practical application. He explains that both the best and the worst experiences work for the good of God's people. He carefully analyses what it means to be someone who 'loves God' and is 'called according to his purpose'. *All Things For Good* provides the biblical answer to the contemporary question: 'Why do bad things happen to good people?'

ISBN 0 85151 478 2
128pp. Paperback

A BODY OF DIVINITY

Thomas Watson

The first book published by the Trust, this has been one of the best sellers and consistently the most useful and influential of our publications. There are several reasons for this:

1. *The subject of the book*. It deals with the foremost doctrinal and experimental truths of the Christian Faith.

2. *The means of instruction used*. It is based on the Westminster Assembly's *Shorter Catechism*, in which the main principles of Christianity that lie scattered in the Scriptures are brought together and set forth in the form of question and answer. This Catechism is unsurpassed for its 'terse exactitude of definition' and 'logical elaboration' of the fundamentals.

3. *The style of the author*. Watson conveys his thorough doctrinal and experimental knowledge of the truth in such an original, concise, pithy, pungent, racy, rich and illustrative style that he is rightly regarded as the most readable of the Puritans.

ISBN 0 85151 383 2
328pp. Large paperback.

THE TEN COMMANDMENTS
ISBN 0 85151 146 5
280pp. Large paperback.

THE LORD'S PRAYER
ISBN 0 85151 145 7
320pp. Large paperback.

These two volumes complete Watson's exposition of the Westminster Shorter Catechism.

THE DOCTRINE OF REPENTANCE

Thomas Watson

A good case could be made out for believing that 'repentance' is one of the least used words in the Christian church today. In a world that will not tolerate the mention of sin, and in churches where it has been defined only in sociological terms, the biblical teaching on repentance has inevitably been ignored. Only occasionally has a book or booklet been published, or a sermon preached, on the theme.

Knowing what repentance is and actually repenting are essential to true Christianity. Jesus Christ himself said that if we do not repent, we will perish! It is vital, therefore, to read and study what Scripture has to say about this theme.

Few better guides have existed in this or any other area of spiritual experience than Thomas Watson. He was a master of both Scripture and the human heart, and wrote with a simplicity and directness that keeps his work fresh and powerful for the twentieth century.

Thomas Watson, minister of St. Stephen's, Walbrook, in the seventeenth century, was one of the leading spiritual guides of his day. He was also the author of *A Body of Divinity, The Ten Commandments, The Lord's Prayer, The Beatitudes* and *All Things For Good*, also published by the Trust.

ISBN 0 85151 521 5
128pp. Paperback.